ASIA-PACIFIC
DEVELOPMENT
JOURNAL

Vol. 23, No. 1, June 2016

United Nations
New York, 2016

ECONOMIC AND SOCIAL COMMISSION FOR ASIA AND THE PACIFIC

ASIA-PACIFIC DEVELOPMENT JOURNAL

Vol. 23, No. 1, June 2016

United Nations publication
Sales No. E.17.II.F.4
Copyright © United Nations 2016
All rights reserved
Manufactured in Thailand
December 2016 – 700
ISBN: 978-92-1-120736-1
e-ISBN: 978-92-1-060087-3
ISSN: 1020-1246
ST/ESCAP/2764

Advisory Board

Editorial statement

The *Asia-Pacific Development Journal* is published twice a year by the Economic and Social Commission for Asia and the Pacific.

Its primary objective is to provide a medium for the exchange of knowledge, experience, ideas, information and data on all aspects of economic and social development in the Asian and Pacific region. The emphasis of the Journal is on the publication of empirically based, policy-oriented articles in the areas of poverty alleviation, emerging social issues and managing globalization.

Original articles analysing issues and problems relevant to the region from the above perspective are welcomed for publication in the Journal. The articles should have a strong emphasis on the policy implications flowing from the analysis. Analytical book reviews will also be considered for publication.

Manuscripts should be sent to:

Chief Editor
Asia-Pacific Development Journal
Macroeconomic Policy and Financing for Development Division
ESCAP, United Nations Building
Rajadamnern Nok Avenue
Bangkok 10200
Thailand
Fax: 66 2 288-3007 or 66 2 288-1000
E-mail: escap-mpdd@un.org

ASIA-PACIFIC DEVELOPMENT JOURNAL
Vol. 23, No. 1, June 2016

CONTENTS

Explanatory notes

References to dollars ($) are to United States dollars, unless otherwise stated.

References to "tons" are to metric tons, unless otherwise specified.

A solidus (/) between dates (e.g. 1980/81) indicates a financial year, a crop year or an academic year.

Use of a hyphen between dates (e.g. 1980-1985) indicates the full period involved, including the beginning and end years.

The following symbols have been used in the tables throughout the journal:

Two dots (..) indicate that data are not available or are not separately reported.

An em-dash (—) indicates that the amount is nil or negligible.

A hyphen (-) indicates that the item is not applicable.

A point (.) is used to indicate decimals.

A space is used to distinguish thousands and millions.

Totals may not add precisely because of rounding.

The designations employed and the presentation of the material in this publication do not imply the expression of any opinion whatsoever on the part of the Secretariat of the United Nations concerning the legal status of any country, territory, city or area or of its authorities, or concerning the delimitation of its frontiers or boundaries.

Where the designation "country or area" appears, it covers countries, territories, cities or areas.

Bibliographical and other references have, wherever possible, been verified. The United Nations bears no responsibility for the availability or functioning of URLs belonging to outside entities.

The opinions, figures and estimates set forth in this publication are the responsibility of the authors and should not necessarily be considered as reflecting the views or carrying the endorsement of the United Nations. Mention of firm names and commercial products does not imply the endorsement of the United Nations.

PUBLIC SPENDING ON HUMAN CAPITAL FORMATION AND ECONOMIC GROWTH IN PAKISTAN

Syed Ammad Ali, Qazi Masood Ahmed and Lubna Naz*

This present paper captures the growth effects of public physical and human capital investment, which highlights the relative efficacy of these types of investments on sectoral and aggregate output, employment and private investment, and indicates which sector of the economy of Pakistan is benefiting the most from these investments. It uses the production function approach based on the Mankiw, Romer and Weil (1992) growth models and applied the Fully Modified Ordinary Least Square (FM-OLS) technique using data from the Pakistan economy during the period 1964-2013. The results show that human capital investment in the public sector has a positive significant effect in all models. The coefficient indicates that a 1 per cent change in human capital investment will increase the output of the manufacturing sector by 0.44 per cent; the output of the services sector by 0.15 per cent; the output of agriculture sector by 0.094 per cent; and the aggregate output by 0.027 per cent. The public physical investment has the highest impact on manufacturing sector output (0.084 per cent) followed by aggregate output (0.034 per cent). The estimated elasticities indicate that at the sectoral level, public human capital investment has a greater output effect than the public physical investment, while at the aggregate level, the public-physical-investment effect dominates.

JEL classification: O40, O53, E62, H40.

Keywords: Economic growth, physical capital, human capital, Pakistan.

*   Syed Ammad Ali, PhD, Research Fellow, Department of Economics University of Karachi (e-mail: ammadsyed@yahoo.com); Qazi Masood Ahmed, PhD, Director, Centre for Business & Economics Research, Institute of Business Administration, Karachi (e-mail: qmasood@iba.edu.pk), and Lubna Naz, PhD, Assistant Professor, Department of Economics, University of Karachi (e-mail: lubnanaz@uok. edu.pk). We acknowledge the reviewers for their valuable comments and suggestions.

I. INTRODUCTION

The differences in growth among the countries initially mainly considered the availability of physical capital stock. However, after the seminal work of Lucas (1988), Romer (1990) and Mankiw, Romer and Weil (1992), the role of human capital in economic growth has become widely accepted, along with the physical capital stock. Human capital stock is determined through education, health, research and development, and training. However, it is still being debated as to which factor is most efficient and effective with regard to human capital accumulation. Another burning issue pertains to the role of public investment. The effectiveness of public investment on private investment and consequently on growth is widely discussed in economic literature. The classical school of thought is of the view that increments in public spending reduces economic growth by crowding out private investment, as higher spending requires higher taxes at individual and corporate levels, which create a distortion in the choice of economic agents. The Keynesians, on the other hand, consider government spending as a key variable for economic growth. They argue that government development expenditures on health, education, and infrastructure increase labour productivity and reduce the cost of conducting business, which spurs gross private domestic investment.

In Pakistan, the public sector is intended to play an effective and efficient role with regard to economic growth and the welfare of the society. In pursuance of these objectives, the Government is trying to improve infrastructure and energy generation and distribution, and promote the establishment of health and education facilities. However, the data trend, as depicted in figure 1, indicates that the ratio of physical investment, the sum of public investment in electricity and gas distribution, and in the transport, storage and communication sector to GDP, and the ratio of human capital investment, the sum of the development expenditures in the health and education sectors to GDP are falling.

The broad objectives of the present study are to test the relative effects of public physical investment and of public human capital investment on economic growth. The effects of public investment are evaluated in three major sectors of the economy, namely the agriculture, manufacturing, and services sectors. This study used the Fully Modified Ordinary Least Square (FM-OLS) technique to measure the long-term relationship between public physical and human capital and economic growth at aggregate and sectoral levels. FM-OLS has several advantages over the previously applied vector error correction model (VECM), ordinary least square (OLS), and autoregressive distributed lag (ARDL) techniques. This study is among a pool very few undertaken in the developing countries that capture the growth effects of public physical and human capital investment. It highlights, in particular, the size of

**Figure 1. Public physical and human capital investment to GDP ratio
in Pakistan**

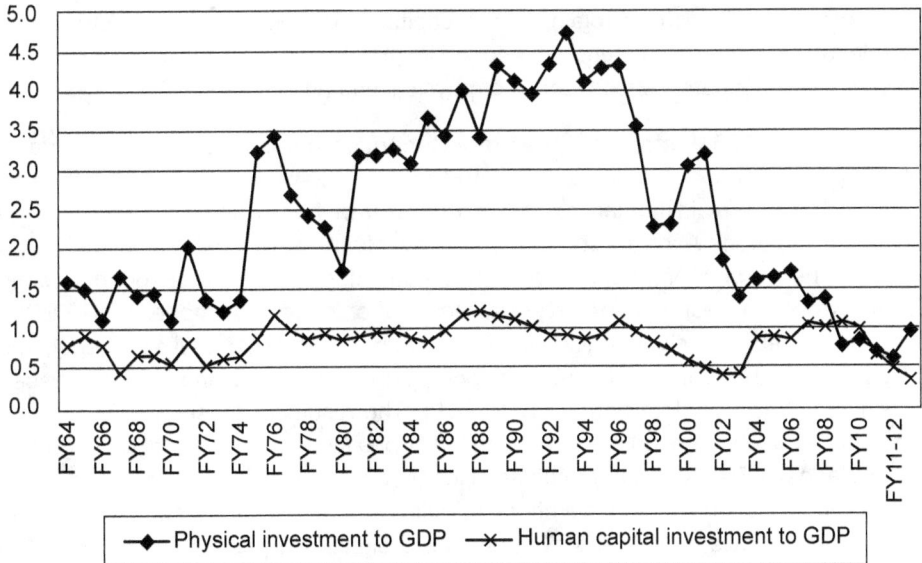

Source: Authors' own estimation based on the data series used for analysis.

the impact of these investments on sectoral and aggregate output growth. Notably, it has some unique features; the definition of human capital for the study as the sum of government health and education development expenditures has never been used before and the definition of physical capital as public investment in the electricity generation and distribution and gas generation and distribution sector plus public investment in the transport, storage and communication sector is also being used for the first time. Furthermore, no other study has examined the relative efficacy of public physical and human capital investment jointly, with exception of one conducted by Khan and Sasaki (2001). However, that study used different proxies for human and physical capital. This study also indicates which sector of the economy of Pakistan is benefiting the most from these investments. All and all, the study provides useful information for policymakers. The remaining section of the study is organized as follows: section II contains a review of past literature, section III provides an explanation of the methodological framework, section IV gives data and a diagnostic test, section V provides the basis for the empirical results and finally the conclusion and policy implications is discussed in section VI.

II. REVIEW OF LITERATURE

The empirical literature related to the research for this study can be divided into three parts: (a) studies on the role of human capital in economic growth; (b) studies on the role of physical investment on economic growth: and (c) research work that explores the comparative effectiveness of physical and human capital.

Schultz (1961) stressed the importance of human capital as a major determinant of economic growth. Many studies that followed then examined the role of public investment in human capital in the form of health and education on the economic situation. A cross-country study by Maitra and Mukhopadhyay (2012) explored the impact of public health and education expenditures on economic growth through a vector autoregressive/vector error correction model (VAR/VECM) for 12 countries, namely Bangladesh, Fiji, Kiribati, Malaysia, Maldives, Nepal, the Philippines, the Republic of Korea, Singapore, Sri Lanka, Tonga and Vanuatu, based on annual time series data from 1981 to 2011. The results of those studies showed that public education spending had a significant positive impact on economic growth in Bangladesh, Fiji, Kiribati, Maldives, Nepal, Singapore, Sri Lanka, Tonga and Vanuatu and a significant negative effect in Malaysia, the Philippines and the Republic of Korea. Meanwhile, health expenditures had a significant positive growth effect in Bangladesh, Nepal, the Philippines, Singapore and Sri Lanka, a significant negative growth effect in Kiribati, Malaysia, Maldives, the Republic of Korea and Vanuatu, and no effect in Fiji and Tonga.

Khan (2005) analysed the impact of human capital on economic growth by applying a cross-sectional regression for 72 low and middle-income countries, including Pakistan, and using the mean value of all selected variables for the period 1980-2002. Another variable used by Khan was average years of schooling, literacy rate, school enrolment and life expectancy at birth, as a proxy for human capital. The results show that the educational and health indicators have a significant positive effect on real per-capita growth. More specifically, in the case of Pakistan, Khan noted that even though human capital investment has been very low compared to other economies in Asia, it has had a significant effect on the country's economic growth rate, which can further be accelerated by increasing the quality of human capital. Tamang (2011) investigated the impact of education expenditures on GDP growth in India through Johansen cointegration on an annual data set covering the period 1980-2008. He found that a 1 per cent increase in public education expenditure per worker will lead to 0.11 per cent increase in GDP per worker. Ogungbenle, Olawumi and Obasuyi (2013) estimated the link among life expectancy, public health spending and economic growth in Nigeria using annual time series data for the period 1977-2008 through a VAR model and found a bi-directional causality between public health spending and economic growth. Hussin, Muhammad and Razak (2012) examined the impact of education expenditures on economic growth in Malaysia using a VECM model with the following variables: GDP; fixed capital formation; labour force participation; and public education expenditures. The results confirm that the education expenditures have Granger causality with GDP growth.

Akram, Padda and Khan (2008) investigated the impact of social capital on economic growth in Pakistan using an annual data series for the period 1972-2006 through a VECM model. The variables included per capita GDP, life expectancy, infant mortality, secondary school enrolment, population per bed and health expenditure as a percentage of GDP. The results show that the health indicators, except for health expenditures, have a significant impact on growth in the long run, but no significant impact in the short run. Abbas and Foreman-Peck (2007) estimated the impact of human capital on economic growth in Pakistan using data from 1960 to 2003 through the Johansen cointegration technique using the secondary enrolment to labour force ratio and health expenditure as a percentage of GDP as a proxy for human capital. They concluded that, among other factors, human capital had a high positive growth effect and that this growth effect was much greater in the case of health expenditure compared to education expenditure. Qadri and Waheed (2011) analysed the impact of human capital on economic growth in Pakistan by using a modified proxy, primary enrolment rate multiplied by expenditures on health as a percentage of GDP. For the study, time series data from 1978 to 2007 and the OLS technique were used. Qadri and Waheed (2011) found a highly significant positive growth effect of this health adjusted human capital.

The impact of physical capital formation through public spending on economic activities has been rigorously analysed in several studies. Pereira (2000) pioneered work in this area by investigating the effects of aggregate public investment and infrastructure investment at a disaggregated level by using a VAR model for the United States of America. He found that at both the aggregated and disaggregated levels, public investment had a positive effect on output and crowd in private investment. The study also showed that marginal productivity was 4.46, indicating that each dollar invested would increase private output by $4.46, the highest rate of return was 16.1 per cent in the electric, gas, transit system and airfield sector.

Fan, Zhang and Zhang (2002) estimated the marginal productivity and returns of different public spending in research and development, irrigation, roads, education, electricity, and telephones in rural China using the panel data (1970-1997) of different provinces of China. The estimated results, based on a simultaneous equations model, indicated that investment in education has the highest marginal productivity among the types of public investment analysed.

Wang (2005) analysed the impact of five different types of government expenditures in Canada: expenditure on protection of persons and property; capital and infrastructure; human capital; debt charges; and expenditure on government and social services on private investment. The study found a significant crowding-out effect of expenditure on capital and infrastructure while expenditure on human capital had a significant crowding-in effect. Murty and Soumya (2006) used a macroeconomic general equilibrium model to investigate the effect of public investment in infrastructure on growth and poverty from 1979 to 2003 in India. The results indicated that a 20 per cent sustained increase in public infrastructure investment finance through borrowing by commercial banks would increase real growth by 1.8 per cent and result in a 0.7 per cent decline in poverty. Pina and Aubyn (2006) examined the rate of return of public investment in the United States using a VAR model for the period 1956-2001. Four variables were used in the model, namely real private investment, real public investment, private employment and real private GDP. The results showed a positive partial-cost dynamic feedback rate of return of 7.33 per cent while the total or full-cost dynamic feedback rate of return was 3.68 per cent.

Marattin and Salotti (2014) estimated the multiplier effect of five different types of public spending on private consumption in the United Kingdom of Great Britain and Northern Ireland through a structural vector error correction (SVEC) model. They conclude that the shock in wages have a negative impact, while total public consumption and social security spending have a positive effect on private consumption. Ocran (2011) investigated the impact of government consumption expenditures, public investment, deficit and revenue on economic growth of South Africa using five different VAR models. The study was based on quarterly data from 1990 to 2004. The results suggest that government consumption expenditures, investment and tax revenue have a significant positive growth effect, with public consumption having the largest growth effect and the deficit having no significant impact on economic growth.

Saeed and Ali (2006) examined the effect of public investment at the aggregate and disaggregate levels in a VAR model using the following real variables: public investment; employed labour force; GDP; and private investment at the aggregate level and for the manufacturing and agriculture sectors. The study found that in agriculture, there was crowding in while in the manufacturing sector, the crowding out effect was prevalent and at the aggregate level, it was inconclusive. Naqvi (2003) analysed the impact of per worker aggregate public and private capital in Pakistan through a VECM model using data from the period 1965-2000. The findings were different under the assumptions of exogenous technological changes and endogenous technological changes. The time trend was used as a proxy of technological change in the model. The results showed that in the exogenous model, the elasticities of private and public capital per workers were 0.25 and 0.23, respectively. In endogenous model the long-term elasticity of public investment is much higher at 0.49 and 0.29, respectively.

Hyder (2001) examined the effect of real public investment on private investment and growth in Pakistan for the period 1964-2001 through a VEC model and found a complementary relationship between public and private investment and a positive growth effect. Khan and Sasaki (2001) analysed the impact of per worker public capital at the aggregated and disaggregated levels on economic growth in seven sectors, including agriculture for Pakistan. This study analysed the impact of public investment on aggregate private investment by using annual data series from 1964 to 1997 through a standard production function approach. The estimated elasticities of public investment at the aggregated and disaggregated levels, employment elasticity and private investment elasticities were positive, while the output elasticities to employment were negative in four of the seven sectors, namely in the energy, transport, communications and services sectors. Ammad and Ahmed (2014) analysed the impact of public energy sector investment on sectoral economic growth, private investment and employment in Pakistan. The estimation was based on VAR methodology covering the data period 1981-2011. They found a strong crowding-in effect of public energy investment, as the effects were positive in seven out of the eight sectors that were analysed, while, in terms of output, the public energy investment also has a positive effect in seven out of the eight sectors.

The existing literature specifically related to Pakistan revealed that different proxies have been used for human capital, such as secondary enrolment rate, health expenditures as percentage of GDP, life expectancy, infant mortality, and social welfare including community services and financial sector facilities. The physical capital stock is measured in terms of public investment in different sectors at the aggregate level, including the agriculture, manufacturing, energy, and transport and communication sectors.

III. THEORETICAL FRAMEWORK AND ECONOMETRIC TECHNIQUE

The objective of the present study is to determine the role of public physical and human capital investment in economic growth of Pakistan. To accomplish this, the production function approach based on Mankiw, Romer and Weil (1992) growth models is applied. It is formulated as follows:

$$Y_{ti} = A_t K_{ti}^{\alpha} H_t^{\beta} L_{ti}^{1-\alpha-\beta} \qquad (1)$$

Where Y is the output of ith sector, which is the function of capital investment in that sector (K_{ti}), human capital (H_t), and labour in that sector (L_{ti}).

Capital investment is further broken up into general private investment, in a particular sector and public physical investment. Finally, an estimate is made of the following linear function after the log transformation of equation 1.

$$LnY_{ti} = C + \alpha LnK_{ti} + \gamma Ln\ L_{ti} + \beta Ln\ H_t + \delta Ln\ Phy_t + \mu \qquad (2)$$

Where lnY_{ti} is the log of real output in particular sector, $C = lnA_t$, $\Upsilon = (1-\alpha-\beta)$, lnK_{ti} is the gross fixed capital formation by private sector in particular sector, lnL_{ti} is the log of employment in the particular sector, lnH_t is the log of real human capital, which is the sum of health and education development expenditures, $lnPhy_t$ is the log of real physical capital investment, which comprises public investment in electricity generation, distribution and gas distribution sector plus public investment in transport, storage and communication sector. Theoretically, the expected signs of estimated coefficients are positive.

To test the long-run relationship between economic growth, public physical and human capital investment, the study employed FM-OLS introduced by Phillips and Hansen (1990). FM-OLS certainly has some significant advantages over other long-run estimation techniques, especially in case of a single cointegrating vector when all the data series are I(1). It also addresses the issues of serial correlation and endogeneity of the regressors; the problem of endogeneity arises when non-stationary series have cointegration links (Phillips, 1991; 1995). Furthermore, FM-OLS is a fully efficient estimation technique for a cointegrating regression even in the presence of different order of integration (Chang and Phillips, 1995). In order to ascertain the applicability of FM-OLS, the Breusch-Godfrey Serial Correlation LM Test was applied on each model, and the Johansen (1991; 1995) approach was used for a number of cointegrating vectors. The results of the Breusch-Godfrey Serial Correlation Lagrang Multiplier (LM) Test are shown in the annex table A.3, which indicates that the OLS estimation results have serial correlation in each of the model, while the cointegration results, mentioned in the annex table A.2 shows that there is only a single cointegrating vector, in each of the models. To incorporate these issues and have efficient long-run estimates, FM-OLS is applied, as discussed by Chang and Phillips (1995) and Phillips and Hansen (1990).

IV. DATA SOURCE AND DESCRIPTION

This study is based on annual time series data from 1964 to 2013 for three major sectors: agriculture, manufacturing, and services[1] and the aggregate economy of the Pakistan. The data series are from the *State Bank of Pakistan Annual Report*, *50 Years of Pakistan Economy*, and various issues of the *Economic Survey of Pakistan*, with the exception of the data on development expenditures on education, which are collected from poverty reduction strategy papers (PRSP) and from Social Policy and Development Centre (SPDC) *Annual Review 2002-2003*. The study converts all nominal variables into real by using the GDP deflator for 2005/06; the common base of 2005/06 deflator series is generated through the standard splicing technique. The different base year deflators' series of 1959/60, 1980/81, 1999/2000 and 2005/06 are thereby combined. Finally, natural logarithm is applied to all variables used in this study.

Univariate analysis

In order to understand the order of integration of the variables and structural break points, if any, the Augmented Dickey-Fuller and Phillips Perron (PP) test is used to check the order of integration. The test results, which are given in the annex table A.1 show that the variables are non-stationary at a level using a 5 per cent confidence interval, however, at a first difference, all the variables are stationary, in that they are I(I). Furthermore, the Schwarz (1978) and Akaike (1974) information criteria are applied for optimal lag length selection.

Cointegration analysis

To apply FM-OLS, it is fundamental that the variables must be cointegrated. For this, a cointegration test is applied to all models by using the Johansen (1991; 1995) approach. The test results, presented in the annex table A.2, show that, in the four models, there is at most one cointegration vector.

Diagnostic test

Two sets of diagnostic tests are applied to retrieve robust results through estimation, one on the long-run estimation results of FM-OLS and one on the short-run estimation results of VECM. The lower part of table 1 shows that the values for R^2 and F-statistics of each model are highly significant. The presence of multicollinearity among exogenous variables is tested through the Coefficient Variance Decomposition

---

[1]   They consist on transport storage and communication, wholesale and retail trade, financial institutions banking and insurance, housing services and general government services.

Table 1. Fully Modified Ordinary Least Square long-run elasticities

Dependent variable ⟶	Aggregate sector	Manufacturing sector	Services sector	Agriculture sector
	Aggregate output	Manufacturing output	Services output	Agriculture output
Explanatory variables ↓	Coefficient (T-ratio) [Prob]	Coefficient (T-ratio) [Prob]	Coefficient (T-ratio) [Prob]	Coefficient (T-ratio) [Prob]
Private investment	0.19* (15.93) [0.00]	0.19* (11.90) [0.00]	0.096* (2.56) [0.014]	0.20* (5.99) [0.00]
Employment	1.58* (41.58) [0.00]	0.48* (10.81) [0.00]	1.31* (15.93) [0.00]	1.281* (8.67) [0.00]
Public physical investment	0.034* (5.24) [0.00]	0.084* (4.94) [0.00]	0.017 (0.97) [0.34]	-0.015 (-0.82) [0.41]
Public human capital investment	0.027** (2.22) [0.031]	0.44* (17.52) [0.00]	0.15* (5.20) [0.00]	0.094* (2.72) [0.00]
Constant	-4.48 (-19.77) [0.00]	1.49 (6.36) [0.00]	-0.67 (-2.53) [0.01]	-1.66 (-1.63) [0.11]
R-squared	0.99	0.94	0.98	0.96
F-statistic	2 004.87	191.45	678.85	321.66

Source: Authors' own estimation.

Notes: *, ** Indicates significance at 1% and 5%, respectively.

test for each model; the results indicate no multicollinearity in each case.[2] Finally, the residual of each model is saved and then the Box-Pierce/Ljung-Box Q-statistics is applied for a residual serial correlation test; the results imply that there is no serial correlation. Another set of diagnostic tests is applied to the vector error correction model (VECM); the results are displayed in the annex table A.5. The diagnostic results indicate that on the basis of the LM test, there is no serial correlation. The heteroskedasticity test shown in the annex table A.5; also confirms that there is no

---

[2]   For the sake of brevity the results are not reported, but are available on demand.

heteroskedasticity. For parameters stability, the AR unit root test is applied[3] which also confirms that all of the roots lie within the unit circle.

V. EMPIRICAL RESULTS

The estimated results, based on long-run elasticities are discussed in the annex table A.1, which is divided into five columns: the first column contains a list of explanatory variables and the remaining four columns represent each model. The results show that private investment has a significant positive effect on output in all four models, at the aggregate level and in the three sectoral models related to the manufacturing, services and agriculture sectors. The estimated coefficient indicates that the highest elasticity is in agriculture sector output (0.2 per cent), followed by manufacturing output (0.19 per cent), aggregate output (0.19 per cent) and services sector output (0.096 per cent) in the case of a 1 per cent change in private investment in the respective sector. In the case of employment, a 1 per cent change in respective employment brings the highest change in aggregate output (1.58 per cent) followed by services (1.31 per cent), agriculture (1.28 per cent) and manufacturing (0.48 per cent).

Physical investment has a positive significant effect on aggregate output and manufacturing output, while it is insignificant in the other two sectors. The coefficients of public physical investment indicates that a 1 per cent change in physical investment results in a 0.084 per cent change in manufacturing output, while in the case of aggregate output it results in a change of 0.034 per cent.

Public human capital has positive significant effect in the four models. The coefficient indicates that a 1 per cent change in human capital investment increases the output of the manufacturing sector by 0.44 per cent, output of the services sector by 0.15 per cent, output of the agriculture sector by 0.094 per cent and the aggregate output by 0.027 per cent. The estimated elasticities indicate that the largest benefit of human capital investment is in the manufacturing sector followed by the services and agriculture sectors. A comparison of the public human and physical capital investment shows that in the sectoral level, public human capital has a larger output effect than the public physical investment. However, at the aggregate level, public physical investment has a larger output effect than public human capital investment.

In addition to the long-run estimation, the VEC model is applied in each case to estimate the short-run dynamics through error correction term (ECT). The results, which are shown in the annex table A.3, indicate that, in all cases, the ECT coefficient

---

[3] Results of the AR Unit root test are given in the annex.

is significant with a theoretical negative sign. This significance also confirms the existence of cointegration. The coefficient of ECT is 29 per cent in the aggregate model, 49 per cent, in the manufacturing model, 54 per cent in the services model and 30 per cent in the agriculture model, for any deviation from equilibrium.

VI. SENSITIVITY ANALYSIS

To test the robustness of the results, especially the sign and magnitude of the estimated elasticities, a sensitivity analysis is performed in which the models are re-estimated after reducing the sample size. The sensitivity results are shown in table 2, which depicts that all the parameters are stable in magnitude, sign and

Table 2. Fully Modified Least Squares long-run elasticities-sensitivity results

Dependent variable ⟶	Aggregate model based on 27 observations	Manufacturing sector model based on 41 observations	Services sector model based on 40 observations	Agriculture sector model based on 36 observations
	Aggregate output	Manufacturing output	Services output	Agriculture output
Explanatory variables ↓	Coefficient (T-ratio) [Prob]	Coefficient (T-ratio) [Prob]	Coefficient (T-Ratio) [Prob]	Coefficient (T-ratio) [Prob]
Private investment	0.13 (4.76) [0.0001]	0.19 (3.21) [0.0028]	0.42 (13.74) [0.0000]	0.04 (0.88) [0.3837]
Employment	0.7 (3.92) [0.0007]	0.92 (4.42) [0.0001]	0.76 (12.04) [0.0000]	2.4 (9.81) [0.0000]
Public physical investment	0.13 (3.68) [0.0013]	0.29 (3.29) [0.0022]	0.01 (0.96) [0.3453]	-0.17 (-4.57) [0.0001]
Public human capital investment	0.22 (4.24) [0.0003]	0.14 (1.1) [0.2806]	0.05 (2.16) [0.0379]	0.18 (3) [0.0053]
Constant	2.21 (1.76) [0.0928]	-1.42 (-1.21) [0.2324]	1.64 (6.65) [0.0000]	-9.91 (-5.69) [0.0000]

significance, with the exception of few deviations. In the agriculture sector, there is a minor deviation in the agriculture sector in which private investment has the same sign but is insignificant while physical investment becomes significant. In the manufacturing model, the sensitivity coefficient of human capital is insignificant, however, it has the same positive sign as in the main model.

VII. CONCLUSIONS AND POLICY IMPLICATIONS

The present study provides some interesting new, which can help policymakers understand better the role of government policy in using public investment as a strategy to boost output in a country. The issue of development priorities is also addressed in this paper; the study results give empirical evidence that physical and human capital investments have a positive impact on the economy whereas human capital investment has more intense effects on output. The sectoral analysis further indicates that public human capital investment has a larger positive significant effect than the public physical investment on sectoral output in the three sectors covered in the study.

The results also support the growth stimulating impact of public investment. However, the Government of Pakistan and the International Monetary Fund have agreed to apply a strategy for economic growth through the private sector in which financing for that sector comes from the banking sector. They are of the view that this is possible after the fiscal deficit is reduced, and the government would need less money from the banking sector to meet its financing needs. This, in turn, would make more money available for the private sector. This strategy assumes that the economy has been facing a crowding-out phenomenon of public investment for private investment. However, in assuming a drastic reduction in the budget deficit, the downward rigidities of current expenditures and upward rigidity of revenue are not considered. In the *Annual Review* of SPDC (2001), an analysis shows that efforts to reduce the fiscal deficit cannot be achieved by cutting non-development expenditures or by increasing tax revenues. In most cases, governments have reduced budget deficits by cutting development expenditures, which then creates shortages in infrastructure and adversely affects private investment. Therefore, based on the experience of the Pakistan economy, proposed reductions in fiscal deficit will lead to the crowding-out effect.

REFERENCES

Abbas, Qaisar, and James Foreman-Peck (2007). Human capital and economic growth: Pakistan 1960-2003. Cardiff Business School Working Papers Series, E2007/22. Cardiff, U.K.: Cardiff University.

Akaike, Hirotugu (1974). A new look at the statistical model identification. *IEEE Transactions on Automatic Control*, vol. 19, No. 6, pp. 716-723.

Akram, Naeem, Ihtsham Ul Haq Padda, and Mohammad Khan (2008). The long term impact of health on economic growth in Pakistan. *Pakistan Development Review*, vol. 47, No. 4, pp. 487-500.

Ammad, Syed, and Qazi Masood Ahmed (2014). Dynamic effects of energy sector public investment on sectoral economic growth: experience from Pakistan economy. *The Pakistan Development Review*, vol. 53, No. 4, pp. 403-420.

Chang, Yooson, and Peter C.B. Phillips (1995). Time series regression with mixtures of integrated processes. *Econometric Theory*, vol. 11, No. 5, pp. 1033-1094.

Dickey, David A., and Wayne A. Fuller (1979). Distribution of the estimators for autoregressive time series with a unit root. *Journal of the American Statistical Association*, vol. 74, No. 3661, pp. 427-431.

Fan, Shenggen, Linxiu Zhang, and Xiaobo Zhang (2002). Growth, inequality, and poverty in rural China: the role of public investments. Research Report, No. 125. Washington, D.C.: International Food Policy Research Institute.

Hussin, Mohd Yahya Mohd, Fidlizan Muhammad, and Azila Abdul Razak (2012). Education expenditure and economic growth: a causal analysis for Malaysia. *Journal of Economics and Sustainable Development*, vol. 3, No. 7, pp. 71-81.

Hyder, Kalim (2001). Crowding-out hypothesis in a vector error correction framework: a case study of Pakistan. *The Pakistan Development Review*, vol. 40, No. 4 (part II), pp. 633-650.

Johansen, Soren (1991). Estimation and hypothesis testing of cointegrating vectors in Gaussian vector autoregressive models. *Econometrica*, vol. 59, No. 6, pp. 1551-1580.

_____ (1995). *Likelihood-based Inference in Cointegrated Vector Autoregressive Models*. Oxford: Oxford University Press.

Khan, M. Tariq Yousuf, and Komei Sasaki (2001). Roles of public capital in Pakistan economy: productivity, investment and growth analysis. *Review of Urban and Regional Development Studies*, vol. 13, No. 2, pp. 143-162.

Khan, Mohsin S. (2005). Human capital and economic growth in Pakistan. *The Pakistan Development Review*, vol. 44, No. 4 (part I), pp. 455-478.

Lucas, Robert E., Jr. (1988). On the mechanics of economic development. *Journal of Monetary Economics*, vol. 22, pp. 3-42.

MacKinnon, James G., Alfred A. Haug, and Leo Michelis (1999). Numerical distribution functions of likelihood ratio tests for cointegration. *Journal of Applied Econometrics,* vol. 14, No. 5, pp. 563-577.

Maitra, Biswajit, and C.K. Mukhopadhyay (2012). Public spending on education, health care and economic growth in the selected countries of Asia and the Pacific. *Asia-Pacific Development Journal*, vol. 19, No. 2 (December), pp. 19-48.

Mankiw, N. Gregory, David Romer, and David N. Weil (1992). A contribution to the empirics of economic growth. *The Quarterly Journal of Economics*, vol. 107, No. 2, pp. 407-437.

Marattin, Luigi, and Simone Salotti (2014). Consumption multipliers of different types of public spending: a structural vector error correction analysis for the UK. *Empirical Economics*, vol. 46, No. 4, pp. 1197-1220.

Murty, K.N., and A. Soumya (2006). Effects of public investment in infrastructure on growth and poverty in India. Working Papers, 2006-006. Mumbai, India: Indira Gandhi Institute of Development Research.

Naqvi, Naveed (2003). Is public capital more productive than private capital? Macroeconomic evidence from Pakistan, 1965-2000. Working Paper in Economics and Finance, No. 03/03. Durham, U.K.: University of Durham.

Ocran, Matthew Kofi (2011). Fiscal policy and economic growth in South Africa. *Journal of Economic Studies*, vol. 38, No. 5, pp. 604-618.

Ogungbenle, S., O.R. Olawumi, and F.O.T. Obasuyi (2013). Life expectancy, public health spending and economic growth in Nigeria: a vector autoregressive (VAR) model. *European Scientific Journal*, vol. 9, No. 19, pp. 210-235.

Pereira, Alfredo M. (2000). Is all public capital created equal? *Review of Economics and Statistics*, vol. 82, No. 3, pp. 513-518.

Phillips, Peter C.B. (1991). Optimal inference in cointegrated systems. *Econometrica*, vol. 59, Issue 2, pp. 238-306.

_____ (1995). Fully modified least squares and sector autoregression. *Econometrica*, vol. 63, No. 5 (September), pp. 1023-1078.

Phillips, Peter C.B., and Bruce E. Hansen (1990). Statistical inference in instrumental variables regression with I(1) processes. *The Review of Economics Studies*, vol. 57, No. 1, pp. 99-125.

Phillips, Peter C.B., and Pierre Perron (1988). Testing for a unit root in time series regression. *Biometrika*, vol. 75, pp. 335-346.

Pina, Alvaro M., and Miguel St. Aubyn (2006). How should we measure the return on public investment in a var? *Economics Bulletin*, vol. 8, No. 5, pp. 1-4.

Qadri, Faisal Sultan, and Abdul Waheed (2011). Human capital and economic growth: time series evidence from Pakistan. *The Pakistan Business Review*, vol. 1, pp. 815-833.

Romer, Paul M. (1990). Human capital and growth: theory and evidence. Carnegie-Rochester Conference Series on Public Policy. *Elsevier*, vol. 32, No. 1 (January), pp. 251-286.

Saeed, Norman, and others (2006). The impact of public investment on private investment: a disaggregated analysis. *The Pakistan Development Review*, vol. 45, No. 4, pp. 639-663.

Schultz, Theodore W. (1961). Investment in human capital. *The American Economic Review*, vol. 51, No. 1 (March), pp. 1-17.

Schwarz, Gideon. (1978). Estimating the dimension of a model. *The Annals of Statistics*, vol. 6, No. 2, (March) pp. 461-464.

Social Policy and Development Centre (SPDC) (2001). *Social Development in Pakistan: Towards Poverty Reduction. Annual Review 2000*. Oxford: Oxford University Press. Available from www.spdc.org.pk/Data/Publication/PDF/AR-3.pdf.

Tamang, Pravesh (2011). The impact of education expenditure on India's economic growth. *Journal of International Academic Research*, vol. 11, No. 3, pp. 14-20.

Wang, Baotai (2005). Effects of government expenditure on private investment: Canadian empirical evidence. *Empirical Economics*, vol. 30, No. 2, pp. 493-504.

ANNEX

Table A.1. Unit root analysis

Variables	Augmented Dickey-Fuller test				Phillips-Perron test			
	Level		1st difference		Level		1st difference	
	With intercept	With trend and intercept	With intercept	With trend and intercept	With intercept	With trend and intercept	With intercept	With trend and intercept
	p-value	p-value	p-value	p-value	p-value	p-value	p-value	p-value
LAGG_GDP	0.8996	0.3046	0*	0*	0.8422	0.2062	0*	0*
LMFG_GDP	0.8209	0.4153	0*	0*	0.7144	0.2429	0*	0*
LSRV_GDP	0.8069	0.3973	0*	0.0002*	0.6836	0.1027	0*	0*
LAGR_GDP	0.9916	0.4334	0*	0*	0.9992	0.5576	0*	0*
LAGG_EMP	0.993	0.535	0*	0*	0.993	0.4834	0*	0*
LAGR_EMP	0.9715	0.1749	0*	0*	0.9951	0.1797	0*	0*
LMFG_EMP	0.9441	0.7146	0*	0*	0.9441	0.6752	0*	0*
LSRV_EMP	0.7515	0.1166	0*	0*	0.6234	0.1141	0*	0*
LAGG_IPRV	0.9633	0.325	0*	0*	0.9591	0.3051	0*	0*
LAGR_IPRV	0.9658	0.3391	0*	0*	0.9754	0.316	0*	0*
LMFG_IPRV	0.8606	0.7351	0*	0.0004*	0.8403	0.6031	0*	0.0004*
LSRV_IPRV	0.9589	0.3913	0*	0.0001*	0.9537	0.3481	0*	0.0001*
LHUMAN	0.2072	0.3088	0.004*	0.0108*	0.48	0.508	0*	0*
LPHYSICAL	0.0319	0.2817	0*	0.0001*	0.1695	0.8063	0*	0*

Notes: *, ** and *** show the stationarity at 1%, 5% and 10% level of significance, respectively.

LAGR is representing the log of agriculture sector, LMFG is the log of manufacturing sector, LSRV is the log of services sector, LAGG is the log of aggregate economy, GDP is the real output, EMP is the employment, IPRV is real private investment, LHUMAN is real human capital investment and LPHYSICAL is the real physical capital investment.

Cointegration test

Table A.2. Johansen cointegration test

Models	Hypotheses	Trace-test	5 per cent critical value	Prob-value**	Hypotheses	Max-Eigen Statistic	5 per cent critical value	Prob-value
Aggregate economy model	$R = 0^*$	97.05	88.80	0.01	$R = 0^*$	38.98	38.33	0.04
	$R \leq 1$	58.07	63.88	0.14	$R \leq 1$	31.01	32.12	0.07
	$R \leq 2$	27.05	42.92	0.68	$R \leq 2$	16.21	25.82	0.53
	$R \leq 3$	10.84	25.87	0.88	$R \leq 3$	6.77	19.39	0.92
	$R \leq 4$	4.07	12.52	0.73	$R \leq 4$	4.07	12.52	0.73
Agriculture sector model	$R = 0^*$	96.62	88.80	0.01	$R = 0^*$	41.91	38.33	0.02
	$R \leq 1$	54.71	63.88	0.23	$R \leq 1$	24.34	32.12	0.33
	$R \leq 2$	30.37	42.92	0.48	$R \leq 2$	20.53	25.82	0.21
	$R \leq 3$	9.84	25.87	0.93	$R \leq 3$	6.05	19.39	0.95
	$R \leq 4$	3.79	12.52	0.77	$R \leq 4$	3.79	12.52	0.77
Manufacturing sector model	$R = 0^*$	99.43	88.80	0.01	$R = 0^*$	39.96	38.33	0.03
	$R \leq 1$	59.47	63.88	0.11	$R \leq 1$	29.61	32.12	0.10
	$R \leq 2$	29.86	42.92	0.51	$R \leq 2$	15.21	25.82	0.62
	$R \leq 3$	14.65	25.87	0.60	$R \leq 3$	11.22	19.39	0.49
	$R \leq 4$	3.44	12.52	0.82	$R \leq 4$	3.44	12.52	0.82
Services sector model	$R = 0^*$	90.10	88.80	0.04	$R = 0^*$	41.51	38.33	0.02
	$R \leq 1$	48.59	63.88	0.48	$R \leq 1$	20.06	32.12	0.65
	$R \leq 2$	28.52	42.92	0.59	$R \leq 2$	13.42	25.82	0.77
	$R \leq 3$	15.10	25.87	0.57	$R \leq 3$	9.27	19.39	0.70
	$R \leq 4$	5.83	12.52	0.48	$R \leq 4$	5.83	12.52	0.48

Notes: R indicates the number of cointegrating vectors.

* Denotes rejection of the null hypothesis at the 0.05 level.

** MacKinnon-Haug-Michelis (1999) p-values.

Table A.3. Pre-estimation test: Breusch-Godfrey Serial Correlation LM

Sectors/model	Autocorrelation test (p-value)
Aggregate model	0.0004*
Agriculture sector model	0.0000*
Services sector model	0.0005*
Manufacturing sector model	0.0000*

Note: *Reject the null hypothesis of "No Serial Correlation".

Table A.4. Short run dynamics error correction representation of the model

Aggregate D(LAGG_GDP)		Manufacturing sector D(LMFG_GDP)		Services sector D(LSRV_GDP)		Agriculture sector D(LAGR_GDP)	
Regressor	Coefficient [T-ratio]	Regressor	Coefficient [T-ratio]	Regressor	Coefficient [T-ratio]	Regressor	Coefficient [T-ratio]
ECT	-0.2916 [-2.31813]	ECT	-0.494212 [-4.52821]	ECT	-0.54105 [-3.35956]	ECT	-0.304575 [-5.27629]
D(LAGG_GDP(-1))	0.207277 [0.93412]	D(LMFG_GDP(-1))	0.118536 [0.84497]	D(LSRV_GDP(-1))	0.34374 [2.06964]	D(LAGR_GDP(-1))	-0.342137 [-2.46200]
D(LAGG_GDP(-5))	-0.005485 [-0.02364]	D(LMFG_IPRV(-1))	-0.093362 [-1.82154]	D(LSRV_IPRV(-1))	-0.065645 [-0.97181]	D(LAGR_IPRV(-1))	0.072631 [2.06719]
D(LAGG_IPRV(-1))	-0.116774 [-1.72041]	D(LMFG_EMP(-1))	-0.191748 [-1.70569]	D(LSRV_EMP(-1))	0.200125 [1.47455]	D(LAGR_EMP(-1))	0.110651 [0.73164]
D(LAGG_IPRV(-5))	-0.030087 [-0.50317]	D(LHUMAN(-1))	0.107708 [2.79401]	D(LPHYSICAL(-1))	0.008635 [0.32424]	D(LHUMAN(-1))	-0.118035 [-3.45447]
D(LAGG_EMP(-1))	-0.195006 [-0.60641]	D(LPHYSICAL(-1))	-0.042871 [-1.41395]	D(LHUMAN(-1))	0.005771 [0.18723]	D(LPHYSICAL(-1))	0.052042 [2.03141]
D(LAGG_EMP(-5))	-0.312531 [-0.99586]	C	0.05228 [4.71332]	C	0.035906 [2.67060]	C	0.056802 [7.08228]
D(LHUMAN(-1))	0.03433 [0.70093]						
D(LHUMAN(-5))	0.012312 [0.36762]						

Table A.4. *(continued)*

	Aggregate D(LAGG_GDP)		Manufacturing sector D(LMFG_GDP)		Services sector D(LSRV_GDP)		Agriculture sector D(LAGR_GDP)	
Regressor	Coefficient	[T-ratio]	Regressor	Coefficient [T-ratio]	Regressor	Coefficient [T-ratio]	Regressor	Coefficient [T-ratio]
D(LPHYSICAL(-1))	0.0004	[0.01464]						
D(LPHYSICAL(-5))	0.0053	[0.18961]						
C	0.062566	[3.01986]						

Notes: LAGR is representing the log of agriculture sector, LMFG is the log of manufacturing sector, LSRV is the log of services sector, LAGG is the log of Aggregate economy, GDP is the output, EMP is the employment, IPRV is private investment, LHUMAN is humac capital investment, and LPHYSICAL is the physical capital investment.

Table A.5. Post estimation diagnostic test

Sectors/model	Numbers of lags	Autocorrelation test (p-value)[1]	Heteroskedasticity test (p-value)[2]
Aggregate model	1,5	0.5615	0.2187
Agriculture sector model	1	0.9936	0.629
Services sector model	1	0.6252	0.318
Manufacturing sector model	1	0.572	0.3154

Notes: [1] Based on VAR residual serial correlation LM test with null no serial correlation.

         [2] VAR Residual Heteroskedasticity Tests. For null hypothesis of no Heteroskedasticity.

Figure A.1. Parameters stability: AR root test

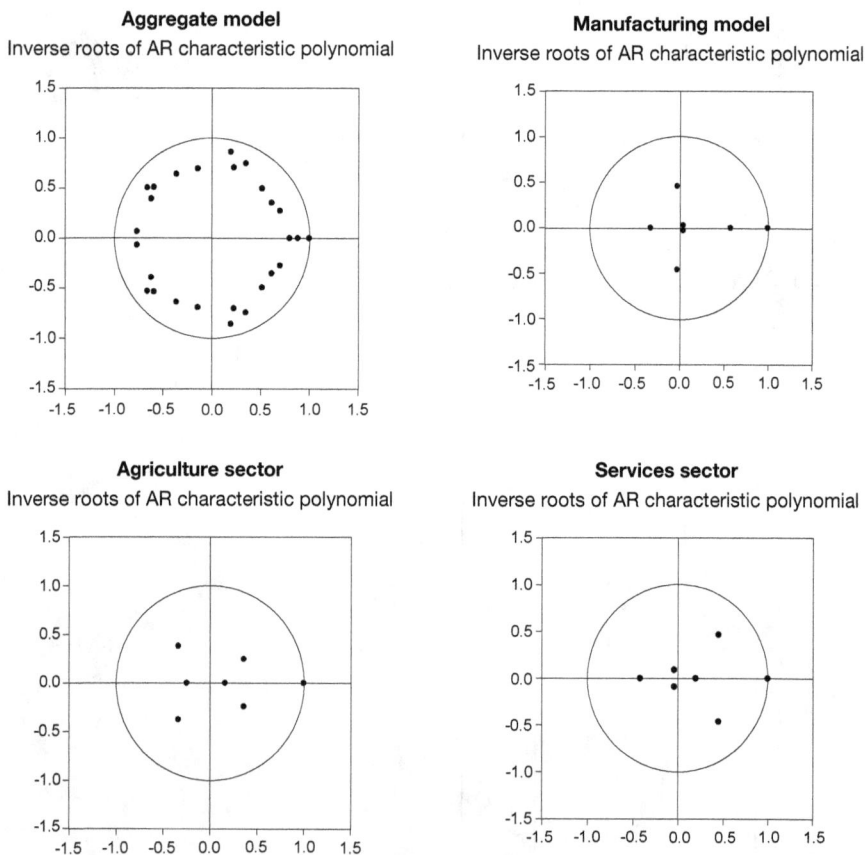

Aggregate model
Inverse roots of AR characteristic polynomial

Manufacturing model
Inverse roots of AR characteristic polynomial

Agriculture sector
Inverse roots of AR characteristic polynomial

Services sector
Inverse roots of AR characteristic polynomial

DOES PRODUCT DIVERSIFICATION AND EMPHASIS ON PROFITABILITY IN MICROFINANCING ALLEVIATE POVERTY?

*Gemunu Nanayakkara and Lokman Mia**

Microfinancing institutions (MFIs) are likely to change their management policies and focus more on profitability and product diversification as they mature and expand in size because of a number of reasons, including among them, donor pressure and/or lack of funding to expand. The present study empirically tests whether such changes occur in MFIs over time and how these changes affect their performance with regard to alleviating poverty.

Using data from a sample of 234 MFIs from around the world, including in the Asia-Pacific region, the study analyses the relationships between age, size, product diversification and emphasis on profitability of MFIs and their impact on the performance in alleviating poverty. Multiple regression techniques and path analysis were used to test the above relationships. The main analysis was also repeated on MFIs in the Asia-Pacific region to assess the relevance of the findings of the main study to the Asia-Pacific region.

Results of the main analysis comprising the 234 MFIs in the sample show that MFIs expand in size with age. As MFIs mature, they diversify to offer other services in addition to providing loans (product diversification). However, size acts as a mediating variable in this relationship. Ageing leads to more emphasis on profitability, which, in turn, leads to an

*   Gemunu Nanayakkara, PhD (Tel: +61 7 37355243; e-mail: G. Nanayakkara@griffith.edu.au); and Lokman Mia, Professor, are from the Department of Accounting, Finance and Economics, Griffith Business School, Griffith University, Brisbane, Qld 4111, Australia. Dr. Nanayakkara is a lecturer at the Griffith University. His research interests include performance of microfinancing institutions and other non-profit organizations. Prof. Mia is a professor at Griffith University. His research interests include performance and organizational behaviour of profit and not-for-profit organizations. He has published papers in many high-level journals, including *Accounting, Organizations and Society*, *Management Accounting Research* and the *British Accounting Review*.

improvement in the performance of MFIs in alleviating poverty. However, product diversification has a negative effect on the performance. The more recently established MFIs, which tend to focus only on providing loans, perform better than older ones (see figure 5).

The analysis, which was repeated only on the 70 MFIs in the Asia-Pacific region, show similar results to those of the main analysis with one exception. The results generally agree with the main findings that as MFIs grow in size with age, they focus more on profitability and adopt product diversification with this transformation. They also agree that emphasis on profitability leads to an improving performance with regard to alleviating poverty. However, the results show that product diversification by MFIs in the Asia-Pacific region has a positive impact on the performance compared with the negative effect found on the main sample.

The findings of this study confirm the shift to commercialism by MFIs over time by emphasizing profitability and product diversification. However, it also indicates that MFIs need be cautious when adopting product diversification strategies.

JEL classification: G21.

Keywords: Product diversification, poverty alleviation, performance, microfinancing.

I. INTRODUCTION

Microfinancing provides loans to the poor who are unable to get credit from commercial institutions, such as banks, because they do not have sufficient income and assets to offer as collateral. After the introduction of this concept by Professor Muhammad Yunus (2001) in the late 1970s, the number of microfinancing institutions (MFIs) has grown rapidly around the world. According to the *State of the Microcredit Summit Campaign Report* completed in 2012, by the end of 2010, there were 3,652 MFIs around the world serving more than 200 million poor people (Reed and Maes, 2012). The phenomenal growth of MFIs has been complemented by hundreds of millions of dollars of donor money injected into the sector. For example, the World Bank has granted US$1.29 billion to MFIs over the years. During 2009 alone, it granted $378 million (World Bank, 2009).

Over the last three decades, MFIs have undergone a number of transformations. Two key areas in this regard pertain to "product diversification" and their "emphasis on profitability". In the early days, MFIs took a non-commercial approach to achieve their objective of alleviation of poverty by only providing loans to the poor with the help of donor funds. However, during the 1990s, MFIs were compelled to take a more commercial focus due to lack of donor funding and donor pressure (Robinson, 2001; 2002; Fernando, 2006; Rogaly, 1996). The main argument in support of this is that donors alone do not have adequate funds to finance the global effort to alleviate poverty and hence MFIs need to generate their own surplus funds to expand and help more poor people. For example, the World Bank, one of the main donors to MFIs, developed a subsidy dependence index, which measured the extent to which a microfinancing institution depended on subsidies and by what percentage it needed to increase its interest rates to be self-funding. A transformation into different levels of commercialism has led some MFIs to focus on profits and product diversification strategies, such as offering savings, insurance and other services to the poor in addition to loans (Aitken, 2010; Khan, 2010). However, these transformations have been criticized on the view that they cause MFIs to drive the borrowers into more debt and poverty (Bateman, 2010) and/or that they drive MFIs away from helping the "poorest of the poor" (Marcus, Porter and Harper, 1999; CGAP, 2001).

In this cross-sectional empirical study, the following is investigated:

(a) Whether changes in the management policies of MFIs in relation to *"product diversification"* and *"emphasis on profitability"* occur over time as MFIs mature (age) and increase in size;

(b) Whether these changes in the management policies contribute to improving the *"performance"* (measured in relation to alleviating poverty in a sustainable manner) of MFIs.

"Product diversification" is defined as diversifying into offering more services in addition to the primary core service of offering loans to the poor. MFIs that adopt *"product diversification"* strategies in their management policies tend to be offering other services, such as savings accounts and insurance products, to the poor, in addition to the primary activity of offering loans.

The *"emphasis on profitability"* is defined as the extent to which a microfinancing institution considers profitability as important in its management policies. This can vary across the spectrum from completely not-for-profit MFIs to highly commercial MFIs, such as banks. This variable is measured by the profit margin, as explained in section III, under Operationalization and measurement of variables.

The *"performance"* of a microfinancing institution can have a number of different meanings. In this study, *"performance"* is defined as the ability of the microfinancing institution to *"alleviate poverty in a sustainable manner"*. To assess this construct, four areas of the MFIs operations are taken into account.

First, the increase in outreach (increase in the number of poor people assisted by the microfinancing institution) and the depth of outreach (how poor these customers are) is taken into account. These two factors are used to determine the effort of the microfinancing institution to reach and assist the poor. Then, the portfolio at risk (PAR), the ratio of bad loans to the total loan portfolio, is used as a proxy to measure the impact that the microfinancing institution has made on the poor people that it has assisted. A higher PAR indicates that a greater proportion of the poor who received assistance from MFIs are unable to repay their loans, which, in turn, worsens their financial situation. Consequently, the assistance has not helped to alleviate the poverty. A lower PAR indicates the opposite. Finally, it is argued that the operations of MFIs must be sustainable because, otherwise, their assistance to the poor would not be in a sustainable manner as defined in this study. Therefore, in this study, the "performance" in relation to alleviating poverty in a sustainable manner is measured by an index (Nanayakkara, 2012) consisting of these four factors, which are explained further in section II, under Age and size of microfinancing institutions, and section III, under Operationalization and measurement of variables.

Findings relating to the two research questions (a) and (b) above will contribute to the existing knowledge of the operations and transformations taking place in MFIs, which will help managers and policymakers to better manage the resources, currently totalling hundreds of millions of dollars, allocated to MFIs in the Asia-Pacific region and the rest of the world.

It may be noted that in relation to (a), no analysis has been done on what factors contribute to the changes in the management policies in relation to emphasis on profitability and product diversification, such as donor pressure or lack of funding. Thus far, studies have only focused on whether those changes do occur in MFIs when they mature and expand in size. This is a limitation in the study. The main reason for omitting this extension is difficulty in measuring and obtaining information on donor pressure and how the MFIs react to the pressure.

The findings of this study contribute to enhancing knowledge in the microfinancing area. First, no empirical studies that have looked at the changes that take place in MFIs when they transform over time and how those changes affect their performance in relation to alleviation of poverty. Second, the study extends the findings of past studies done in other industries to microfinancing. For example, a number of studies have looked at the relationship between age, size and product diversification in other industries (Donaldson, 1982; Dass, 2000; Dawley, Hoffman and Brockman, 2003; Geiger and Cashen, 2007). The validity of these findings in microfinancing has been tested. Third, also tested was whether Gibrat's Law explained under section II (Gibrat, 1931), which was later found not to be applicable to certain industries (Evans, 1987; Hall, 1987; Almus and Nerlinger, 1999), is applicable to microfinancing. The results indicate that Gibrat's Law is valid to microfinancing.

The next sections of this paper are organized as follows. Section II covers the literature review. This section looks at the issues surrounding the concept of "performance" in relation to microfinancing. Then, the literature relating to the effect of the independent variables on the performance is discussed to develop the hypotheses. Section III describes the statistical methods used in the analyses. The data collection, operationalization and measurement of variables and relationships between the independent variables are also explained in this section. Analysis of data and results are covered in section IV. Finally, a discussion of the results and the conclusions are given in section V.

II. LITERATURE REVIEW

This section begins with a review of the literature that assesses the various methods used to measure the "performance" of MFIs and then argues the reasons for selecting the method adopted by Nanayakkara (2012). This is followed by the development of the hypotheses in relation to the research questions stated earlier.

Performance of microfinancing institutions

The fundamental aim of MFIs is to help and improve the quality of life of the poor by offering loans without security. This is quite different from that of commercial institutions, such as banks, in which profits take precedence over humanitarian or social factors. Therefore, the achievements or performance of MFIs cannot be measured by indicators used to measure the performance of commercial enterprises, such as profit, increase in share value or return on investment.

Most of the research done shortly after MFIs were introduced looked at their impact on poverty alleviation. These studies focused on measuring the improvement of various social and financial indicators of the poor borrowers as a result of receiving the loans from MFIs. Hulme and Mosley (1996) studied the improvement in income of 4,000 borrowers compared with control groups across four countries and concluded that microfinancing actually alleviates poverty. A number of social indicators, such as health and infant mortality, children's education, nutritional adequacy and attainment of food security, have been used to assess the performance of MFIs in other studies (see Foundation for Development Corporation, 1992; Pitt and Khandker, 1996; Khandker, Khan and Khalily, 1995; Khandker and Khalily, 1996; ADB, 2000; Dunford, 2001; CGAP, 2002). These studies have all confirmed that microfinancing helps to improve the income and quality of life of the poor.

In a number of other studies, the focus had shifted from the impact on the poor borrowers to the efficient internal operations and delivery of service by MFIs. For example, Yaron (1992) found that a large number of MFIs were heavily dependent on subsidies and were not operating efficiently. This was also supported by various other studies (Christen, 1998; Adams, 1998). These studies implied the extent to which MFIs depend on subsidies as a measure of efficiency or "performance" of MFIs and that MFIs needed to generate their own funds by taking a commercial approach. This concept was further extended and quantified by the World Bank when it created an index referred to as the "Subsidy Dependence Index" (SDI) for MFIs. This index measures the extent to which a microfinancing institution depends on subsidies and by what percentage it needs to increase its interest rates to be self-funding. The above studies highlight the importance of both external (impact on alleviating poverty) and internal (operational efficiency) factors when assessing the performance of MFIs. Both dimensions must be included when determining the "performance" of MFIs.

The Consultative Group to Assist the Poor (CGAP) is an international organization funded by more than 20 major donors that support microfinancing. The objective of CGAP is to develop and assist the microfinancing sector around the world. In its guidelines to donors, CGAP (2003) recommends five indicators to be used to assess the performance of a microfinancing institution: portfolio quality; financial sustainability; operational efficiency; outreach; and depth of outreach.

Nanayakkara (2012) has developed an index considering four dimensions to assess the performance of MFIs in relation to poverty alleviation. The first two are the "increase in outreach" (the increase in the number of poor people that the microfinancing institution has assisted over a given period) and the "depth of outreach" (how poor these people are). These two dimensions measure the efforts of MFIs to alleviate poverty in its environment. The third dimension, PAR, indicates the loans that are granted by the microfinancing institution, which are in default now. Although this may be viewed as internal to the microfinancing institution, Nanayakkara (2012) argues that this is a proxy for measuring the impact on the life of the poor as a result of providing the loans. As explained above, a higher PAR indicates that a greater proportion of the poor who receive loans is buried more in debt and poverty. A lower PAR indicates the opposite. The fourth dimension is, "sustainability". Nanayakkara (2012) argues that it is very important that a microfinancing institution be sustainable in order to survive and continue to help alleviate poverty.

One of the main advantages of this index is that it is not bias against such variables as size, country and exchange rates and looks at the external impact made by the microfinancing institution in alleviating poverty, as well as internal operations. This index, given in section III, under Operationalization and measurement of variables, is used in this study to measure a microfinancing institution's "performance" in relation to alleviation of poverty.

Age and size of microfinancing institutions

Age and size are fundamental drivers that create changes in the activities of MFIs. For example, over time (age), MFIs gain knowledge and experiences in the local market pertaining to the type of potential services to offer, as well as become knowledgeable about the expectations of their donors (donor pressure on MFIs to generate their own funds by emphasizing profitability) and borrowers (demanding additional services for product diversification), which can trigger changes to their internal management policies and operations. As MFIs expand, they gain access to more resources needed to implement these changes to their operations. Consequently, age and size serve as fundamental drivers of organizational change. Their impact on the performance is discussed below.

Age and the performance of microfinancing institutions

Several studies have looked at the relationship between the age and the growth rates of commercial companies. Studies conducted by Wagner (1995) and Glancey (1998) on manufacturing firms in Europe have shown that there is a negative relationship between the age and the rate of growth of companies. Using Australian data, Wijewardena and Tibbits (1999) have found that older firms expand at a slower rate compared with newer ones. These findings have also been confirmed by Almus and Nerlinger (1999) when they analysed the growth rates and age of German companies in a longitudinal study spanning over ten years.

However, there is no evidence in the current literature of any detailed studies relating to the relationship between the age and the performance of MFIs. It is difficult to conclude whether the above findings relating to commercial organizations are applicable to MFIs in a similar manner. Commercial organizations have profit as one of their main objectives and obviously private investors set up new companies when they see a significant potential to reap profits with a high certainty in the immediate future. Therefore, in the early days, these companies are likely to make profits, which are used to help them to expand rapidly with the objective to recover their initial costs to achieve the scale of optimum efficiency. However, as time goes by, the initial environment can change and lucrative market opportunities may disappear as the result of competition and changes in other environmental factors. Hence, in the case of commercial organizations, young companies may perform better than mature companies.

However, in contrast, in the case of MFIs, upon inception, profitability is not the main objective. Most MFIs are funded by aid from donors. Therefore, the availability of donor funds (which may depend on lot of other factors) in the early stages may become a major governing factor in the expansion of relatively new MFIs. Another aspect that is worth noting is that because microfinancing is a relatively new area, most mature MFIs may have learned their best practices the hard way, by experimenting with new ideas and procedures. In the case of newly established MFIs, they have the opportunity to learn from the mistakes made by older ones. However, the relationship between age and performance in MFIs has not been investigated in the literature. Following the previous studies in commercial organizations mentioned above, this study hypothesizes an inverse relationship between these two variables. Therefore, the first hypothesis to be tested empirically is stated as follows:

H_1: There is an inverse relationship between age and performance of an microfinancing institution.

Size and the performance of microfinancing institutions

The relationship between the firm size and growth is found in economic theory. Gibrat's Law states that there is no relationship between the size of a firm and its growth rate (Gibrat, 1931). However, a number of subsequent empirical studies have shown that Gibrat's Law does not apply to certain industries. For example, Evans (1987), using data from the United States of America, has shown that smaller firms have higher growth rates. This was further supported by Hall (1987), which used data relating to United States manufacturing companies. Similar findings have been reported in Germany (Almus and Nerlinger, 1999). The above studies are related to manufacturing industries.

However, research carried out in the Netherlands on the service industry has shown that Gibrat's Law is valid for the service industry (Audretsch and others, 2002). A study covering the service sector in Italy has shown mixed results with regard to Gibrat's law (Piergiovanni and others, 2002). The research looked at different business sectors in the hospitality industry and found that while growth was independent of size for some business sectors, Gibrat's Law did not apply for the other businesses that were included in the study. Therefore, the existing literature suggests that, contrary to Gibrat's Law, a relationship between growth and size may exist in some industry sectors.

Does Gibrat's Law apply to the microfinancing institutions, a service industry? In the current literature, no study answers this question. Generally, large organizations have the advantage of a good reputation, which helps them in many ways, including giving them easier access to external funds. They have more resources at their disposal and are less vulnerable to external unforeseen "shocks". Obviously, a larger size itself is a testimony to the fact that the organization has performed well and had expanded at some stage. However, as MFIs are quite different from commercial organizations, the size of a microfinancing institution cannot necessarily be equated to performance. When organizations become large, the span of control expands, which necessitates the introduction of rigid rules, manuals and procedures. Flexibility and being closer to the market to understand the needs of the poor plays a critical role in providing microfinancing services. Early attempts by donors to channel funds through large state banks failed because of the lack of the above factors (Schmidt and Zeitinger, 1994). Small organizations may be closer to the poor borrower, which enables them to have a better understanding of the type of services required by the target market. Owing to the narrow span of control, as a result of the smaller size, the systems and procedures of a small microfinancing institution may be more flexible than a larger microfinancing institution.

"The larger an organization the more formalized its behaviour" (Mintzberg and Quinn, 1998).

Data relating to a study comparing the customer base of nine banks that expanded to provide microfinancing services indicate some interesting results (Valenzuela, 2002). This study found that small MFIs (defined as having fewer than 7,500 customers) have increased their customer base at a much higher rate than that of larger MFIs.

Therefore the second hypothesis to be tested in this study is stated as:

H_2: There is an inverse relationship between the size and the performance of a microfinancing institution.

Management policy on profitability and product diversification

Product diversification

While the management policy of some MFIs is to only focus on providing loans, others offer additional services, such as savings facilities and insurance, to the poor. There are advantages and disadvantages to providing these additional services. For example, in most countries, taking savings deposits requires adhering to stringent regulations and reporting requirements of respective central banks (or reserve banks) in the country. This increases the administration costs to MFIs (Vogel, 1998). However, the problem is that in the absence of a powerful regulatory authority, what guarantees the savings of the poor depositors? Whether the increase in administration costs is outweighed by the gains from deposits is not clear because unlike in commercial banks, the size of the deposits made by the poor is very small.

Vogel (1984) argues that offering savings facilities and other services helps MFIs to become financially viable. He cites successful MFIs, such as BRI (Indonesia), Banco Sol (Bolivia) and ACEP (Senegal), as real world cases to strengthen the argument. There is support for this argument from six case studies presented by Owens and Wisniwiski (1999), who concluded that poor people have both the capacity and the desire to save and that it is impediments in the policies and instruments that inhibit the mobilization of savings rather than the poor people's savings preferences. Savings also open a new avenue for MFIs to access additional funds to expand their customer base. This study examines the impact of product diversification on the performance of MFIs by comparing the performances of MFIs that provide only loans with MFIs that provide other services in addition to loans.

Therefore, the third hypothesis to be tested empirically can be stated as:

H_3: The performance of a microfinancing institution that provides savings facilities and other related services in addition to loans (product diversification) is better than the performance of a microfinancing institution that provides only loans.

Emphasis on profitability

The question of whether MFIs should focus on profits when the objective to alleviate poverty is not very clear. Obviously, emphasis on profitability would generate surplus funds for the microfinancing institution to expand its operations without relying on donors for subsidies. A number of scholars support this view (see Christen, 1998; Robinson, 1998; Schmidt and Zeitinger, 1994). However, the counter argument is that emphasis on profitability would result in MFIs charging higher interest rates to the poor borrowers and the tendency of focusing on the "not-so-poor" borrowers at the expense of the "very poor" borrowers. Therefore, some argue that this would make it difficult for the "poorest of the poor" to access microfinancing services (Marcus, Porter and Harper, 1999). Case studies carried out in Latin America have shown that the not-for-profit MFIs concentrate on the very poor compared to MFIs with a commercial focus (CGAP, 2001).

While the current debate looks at the pros and cons of a commercial focus (high emphasis on profitability) compared with a welfare focus (not-for-profit), it is not known which approach results in improving the overall performance of a microfinancing institution with regard to alleviating poverty, as defined in this study earlier and argued by Nanayakkara (2012). Under the commercial approach, profits generate surplus funds that enable a microfinancing institution to be sustainable and to expand its customer base. This, in turn, improves its ability to reach more poor people. Considering the above factors the fourth hypothesis that is tested empirically in this study can be stated as:

H_4: There is a positive relationship between the emphasis on profitability and the performance of a microfinancing institution.

III. METHOD

The statistical methods used for empirically testing the above hypotheses, operationalization and measurement of variables, the sample and data collection are covered in this section. The analysis that investigates the relationship between the variables mainly consists of two stages. In the first stage the above-mentioned four hypotheses are tested by using multiple regression. The second stage involves testing for any indirect or mediating effects among the independent variables. This is done by using the Baron and Kenny (1986) method, which is outlined in section III, under Testing for indirect and mediating effects.

Hypotheses testing

The four hypotheses developed in section II were tested using multiple regression analysis and the standard equation can be written as follows.

$$\text{Performance} = \beta_0 + \beta_1 \, (\text{Age}) + \beta_2 \, (\text{Size}) + \beta_3 \, (\text{Providing only loans})$$

$$+ \beta_4 \, (\text{Emphasis on profitability}) + \epsilon \qquad (1)$$

Where β_i - Regression coefficients (i = 0, 1, 2...n)

ϵ - Standard error term.

If a particular regression coefficient (β_i) is zero in the formula (at a given confidence level which is taken as the standard 95 per cent in this study), then it can be concluded that the corresponding independent variable has no impact on the dependent variable and vice versa. This forms the basis of testing the four hypotheses.

Testing for indirect and mediating effects

Although some of the independent variables may not have a direct impact on the dependent variable, they can have an indirect or mediating effect through other independent variables. This was tested by using the Baron and Kenny method (1986) outlined below.

Baron and Kenny (1986) method for assessing mediating effects

Figure 1. Relationship of a mediating variable

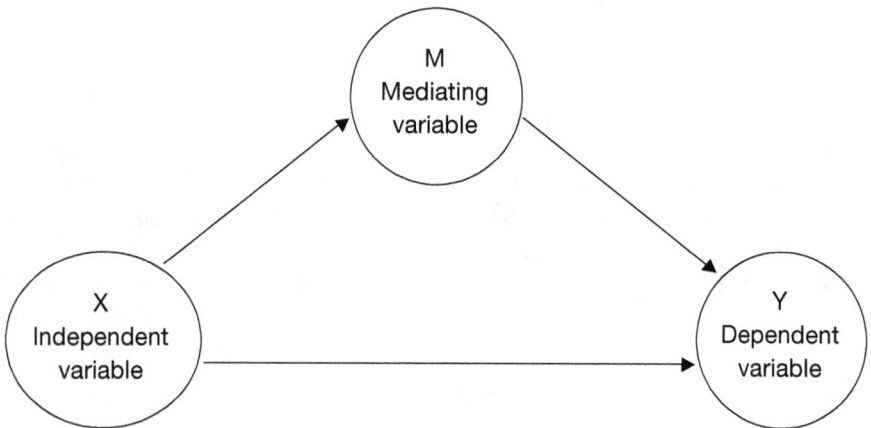

The relationships between the variables are shown in figure 1 where M is the mediating variable. First the following two regressions are run.

$$Y = \beta_{01} + \beta_{11} X + e_1 \tag{2}$$

$$M = \beta_{02} + \beta_{12} X + e_2 \tag{3}$$

where β_{11} – is the impact of X on Y

β_{12} – is the impact of X on M.

If β_{11} is not equal to zero (X influences Y) and β_{12} is also not equal to zero (X influences M) at $p < 0.05$ confidence levels, then possible mediation effects through M are tested by the following equation (note that if $\beta_{12} = 0$ then X does not influence M, and hence there is no mediation).

$$Y = \beta_{03} + \beta_{13} X + \beta_{23} M + e_3 \qquad (4)$$

where β_{13} – is the impact of X on Y after controlling for M

β_{23} – is the impact of M on Y after controlling for X.

If $\beta_{13} = 0$ and β_{23} is not equal to zero at $p < 0.05$ confidence level, then full mediation exists. That is total impact of X on Y shown by β_{11} in the first regression flows through M to Y.

If both β_{13} and β_{23} are not zero at $p < 0.05$ confidence level, then partial mediation exists. That is X still has some direct effect on Y apart from what flows through M to Y.

Using the above method developed by Baron and Kenny (1986), the indirect and mediating effects of the relationships discussed below were tested under this stage.

R_1 – Relationship between the age, size and providing only loans

It is argued at as MFIs become older, they may grow in size. One of the reasons for this is that demand for microfinancing services far exceeds the supply (seller's market). For example, according to the *State of the Microcredit Summit Campaign Report* completed in 2012, only 200 million poor people are served by MFIs around the world compared with 900 million poor in the Asia-Pacific region alone.

There is also evidence that average size of firms increases with age in some industries. For example in the Hutchinson, Patrick and Walsh (2010) study, when kernel density estimates of the firm size distributions were plotted by age cohorts, as firms grow older, the size distribution shifts more to the right. This means that average firm size increases with age. This supports the similar result in the Cabral and Mata (2003) study, which analysed the firm size distributions with age of Portuguese manufacturing companies. Results of some other studies also show a positive significant correlation between firm size and age (Baker and Cullen, 1993; Yasuda, 2005).

It is also argued that both age and size of a microfinancing institution are related to product diversification. A number of studies indicate both age and size have positive effects on the management decision to diversify into other products. Dass (2000), who studied a sample of 555 companies in the United States over a range of industries from mining to manufacturing and services, found that firm size had a significant effect on diversification. Wheeler and others (1999) analysed the determinants of diversification of 3,986 hospitals in the United States into sub-acute care. They found that large hospitals or size had a positive effect on diversification. Studies by Donaldson (1982), Dawley, Hoffman and Brockman (2003) and Geiger and Cashen (2007) also showed that large firms tended to be more inclined to diversify than small ones. In the banking and finance area, Silverman and Castaldi (1992, p. 49) found that: *"Larger community banks were significantly more interested in diversification strategies than their smaller counterparts".*

With age, firms gain more experience and knowledge about the market and related other products that it could potentially offer. This forms the basis for companies to venture into new products and markets related to its existing status quo (Farjourn, 1994; Montgomery and Hariharan, 1991; Chang, 1996; Ingram and Baum, 1997). Therefore, age plays an important role in the ability and the potential of a firm to diversify into related products. Jiang (2006) analysed the determinants of diversification of 895 listed companies in China and found that both the age and size have a significant influence on diversification.

Considering the above, it can be concluded that age has a positive relationship with the size and that both the age and size have significant effects on the ability and the decision of MFIs to diversify into other products, such as savings and insurance, in addition to loans. These relationships are shown in figure 2 and were tested using the Baron and Kenny (1986) method.

R_2 – Relationship between age, emphasis on profitability and performance

Various studies have indicated a trend among MFIs to start as not-for-profit organizations, such as non-governmental organizations (NGOs), and then transform gradually to commercial enterprises (Schmidt, 2010). Case studies carried out in a number of countries in Africa, South America and the Indian subcontinent have confirmed this "mission drift" of MFIs (see Drake and Rhyne, 2002; Rhyne, 2001; Sriram, 2010; Khan, 2010). The reasons behind this trend are explained by Epstein and Yuthas (2010) as follows:

> Like other social enterprises, dependence on funding can push MFIs to become more innovative and entrepreneurial (Mort, Weerawarden and Carnegie, 2003), or it can make them behave more like market-driven corporations (Eikenberry and Kluver, 2004). As the microfinance industry matures, funders are becoming more demanding in their expectations for effective investment of these funds and for clear demonstrations of social impact. Such institutional changes have pushed non-profits toward a corporate approach (Bruck, 2006).

Considering the above, it can be argued that as MFIs mature, they tend to focus more on profitability. Since, it has already been hypothesized that age and emphasis on profitability can have a direct impact on performance, the relationship among these three variables can be shown in figure 4 and was tested using the Baron and Kenny (1986) method described above.

The analysis and results of the above models tested under the Baron and Kenny method are discussed in section IV, under Analysis of mediating effects.

Operationalization and measurement of variables

The variables in the hypotheses at the conceptual level have to be operationalized and measured prior to using them to run the regressions to test the hypotheses. This is discussed below.

Performance

The performance (P*) is operationalized and measured by an indicator comprising the four dimensions as follows. This indicator measures the MFIs performance in relation to "alleviation of poverty in a sustainable manner" as explained previously (Nanayakkara, 2012).

$$P^* = C^* + S^* + [\,1 - D^*\,] + [\,1 - PAR^*\,] \tag{5}$$

Where P* – Performance of the MFI during the period under study

C* – Increase in outreach

D* – Depth of outreach

PAR* – Portfolio at risk greater than 30 days, and

S* - Sustainability.

Age

Age relates to the number of years that the microfinancing institution has operated from the time of inception until the beginning of the year in which its performance was assessed in the study.

Size

The number of employees is argued as the best proxy for determining the size of a microfinancing institution. This is because microfinancing is not a machine-intensive high-tech operation, but, instead, entails carrying out tasks requiring a number of employees (for example, screening loan applications, disbursement of loans and collection of repayments). Therefore, it is reasonable to expect the number of employees to rise when the scale of operation and the size of MFIs increase.

Product diversification

This was measured by categorizing MFIs into two groups using dummy variables, as follows:

LOANS - MFIs that provide only loans (if only loans then value = 1, otherwise zero)

SAVINGS - MFIs that provide savings and other related services in addition to loans. These are MFIs that have gone into product diversification (if loans and other services then value = 1, otherwise zero).

SAVINGS (product diversification) is taken as the base variable and therefore only LOANS is included in the regression.

Emphasis on profitability

The emphasis placed by MFIs on profitability is operationalized and measured by the profit margin made by each microfinancing institution. It can be argued that MFIs that place greater emphasis on profitability have higher profit margins. For example, the profit margin can be easily manipulated by the interest rate charged on the loans by the microfinancing institution. Unlike commercial banks, which are subject to market forces and stiff competition, interest rates are almost totally under the control of MFIs, owing to lack of competition and the high demand compared with the supply of microfinancing services (a seller's market). Therefore, MFIs that place greater emphasis on profitability are likely to have higher profit margins because they can charge higher interest rates.

The profit margin for MFIs is defined by CGAP (2003) as the ratio of net operating income to operating revenue.

Sample and data collection

Data relating to the performance of MFIs were collected from the CGAP-funded mix-market database. The sample size totalled 234 MFIs across 63 countries, including countries in the Asia-Pacific region. The sample also included all types of MFIs (NGOs, cooperatives/credit unions, rural banks, non-bank financial institutions and banks) for which there were data required for the study in the database. The performance varied from -4.56 to 6.8, with an average of 2.8. The size measured by the number of employees ranged from 4 to 18,926. The average size was 306 employees. The average age of MFIs in the sample was 10 years, with the newest one operating only one year and the oldest one functioning for 40 years. Therefore, there was adequate variance and the sample size in the variables was sufficient to support generalizing and extending the findings to all types of MFIs in the Asia-Pacific region and in the rest of the world.

IV. DATA ANALYSIS AND RESULTS

Data screening

The data were first screened to assess the distributions, outliers and missing values. This resulted in the elimination of six cases from the data sample. The distributions of the variables "age" and "size" were positively skewed. This was overcome by creating two additional variables (LAGE & LSIZE) doing a log transformation as follows.

$$LAGE = \log_e (Age) \tag{6}$$

$$LSIZE = \log_e (Size) \tag{7}$$

The distribution of "performance" and "profit margin" did not show any skewness and hence, a log transformation was not required.

Hypotheses testing

This section describes the analysis undertaken to test the four hypotheses developed in section II. All calculations relating to statistics were completed using the SPSS Version 20 software. The correlation matrix is given in table 1.

The results of the regression (ref equation (1) in section III, under Hypotheses testing), which test the four hypotheses, are given in table 2. The significance levels relating to the standardized coefficients of the independent variables shown in table 2 indicate that "emphasis on profitability", "providing only loans" and "age" have a direct significant effect on the "performance" of MFIs at a 95 per cent confidence interval (*$p < 0.05$). However, the effect of "size" on the performance of MFIs is not statistically significant ($p > 0.05$). Therefore, hypothesis H_2 is not supported.

Table 1. Correlation matrix

Variables	Performance	Emphasis on profitability	Providing only loans	Size	Age
1. Performance	1.00				
2. Emphasis on profitability	0.29**	1.00			
3. Providing only loans	0.14*	-0.08	1.00		
4. Size[a]	-0.21	0.01	-0.23**	1.00	
5. Age[a]	-0.08*	0.24**	-0.16*	0.36**	1.00

Notes: [a] Log transformations were used.

Sample N = 234; cross-sectional data.

$*p < 0.05$, $**p < 0.01$.

Table 2. Regression results[a] of equation (1)

Independent variables	Unstandardized coefficient (B)	Standard error	Standardized coefficient (β)
Emphasis on profitability	1.25	0.26	0.31**
Providing only loans	0.31	0.14	0.15*
Size[b]	0.03	0.05	0.03
Age[b]	-0.18	0.11	-0.11*

Notes: [a] Dependent variable – Performance.

[b] Log transformations were used.

$*p < 0.05$, $**p < 0.01$.

Sample N = 234; cross-sectional data.

As shown in table 2, the sign of the regression coefficient for "age" is negative. This indicates that there is a significant inverse relationship between the age and the performance of MFIs. Therefore, hypothesis H_1 is supported.

The sign of "emphasis on profitability" on "performance" is positive, i.e. MFIs perform better if they focus on profitability. In other words, taking a "commercial" approach rather than a "welfare" approach enables MFIs to perform better in alleviating poverty. Hence, the hypothesis H_4 is supported.

The impact of "providing only loans" on the performance is significant ($p < 0.05$). However, the sign of the regression coefficient is positive, which is unexpected. This means that MFIs that only focus on providing loans (no product diversification) perform better than those that have diversified to provide other services in addition to loans. This is opposite to what was hypothesized in H_3 and challenges the findings of previous studies conducted in other industries.

The above results are discussed in detail under section V.

Analysis of mediating effects

This section analyses the mediating effects that were outlined in section III, under Testing for indirect and mediating effect.

R_1 – Relationship between age, size and providing only loans

The relationship between age, size and providing only loans discussed in section III, under Testing for indirect and mediating effect, is shown in figure 2.

Figure 2. Relationship R_1

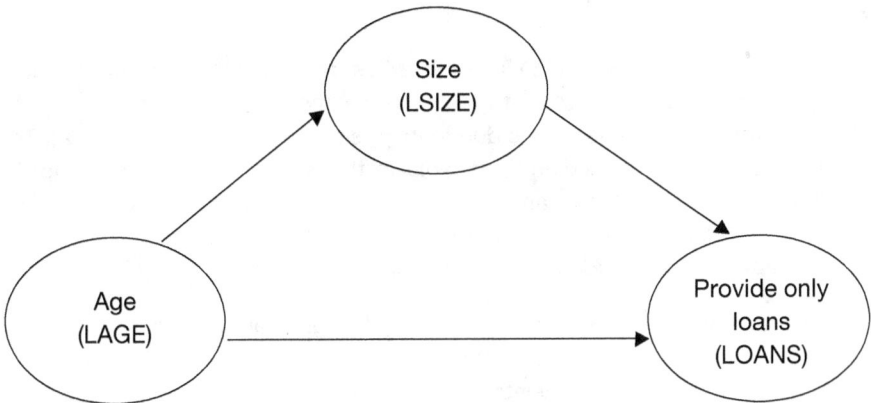

First, regressions were run on "providing only loans" and "size" as dependent variables and age as the independent variable. Then, to test the mediating effect, a regression is run on "providing only loans" as the dependent variable and both "age" and "size" as independent variables (Baron and Kenny method explained in section III, under Testing for indirect and mediating effect). The outputs of these regressions are shown in table 3.

In the results of the first two regressions shown in table 3, "age" has statistically significant relationships with "size" and "providing only loans" (**$p < 0.01$

Table 3. Relationship between age,[a] size[a] and providing only loans

Regression models	β	Value of β_{ij}
Providing only loans = $\beta_{01} + \beta_{11}$ Age + e_1	β_{11}	-0.16**
Size = $\beta_{02} + \beta_{12}$ Age + e_2	β_{12}	0.36**
Providing only loans = $\beta_{03} + \beta_{13}$ Age + β_{23} Size + e_3	β_{13}	-0.11
	β_{23}	-0.19**

Notes: [a] Log transformations were used.

*p < 0.05, **p < 0.01.

Sample N = 234; cross-sectional data.

for β_{11} and β_{12}). The sign of the coefficient for β_{12} is positive. The positive relationship between those two variables means that when MFIs mature, they grow in size, which is expected. The relationship between "providing only loans" and "age" is negative ($\beta_{11} < 0$). This indicates that as MFIs mature, they do **not** "provide only loans"; they also provide other services. In other words, mature MFIs go into product diversification.

Because "age" has a significant positive relationship with "size" (table 3, second regression), it is necessary to test whether the total or part of the effect that age has on product diversification is due to its positive relationship with "size". That is whether "size" acts as a mediating variable in the relationship between "age" and "providing only loans". This is analysed in the third regression when the effect of "age" on "providing only loans" is controlled for the effect of "size" by including both "age" and "size" as independent variables (table 3, third regression).

This regression shows that there is a highly significant negative effect of "size" on "providing only loans" (**p < 0.01 for β_{23}). This means that large MFIs do **not just** "provide only loans" and diversify into other services (product diversification).

The third regression also shows that when "size" is included, the relationship between "age" and "providing only loans" is not significant (p > 0.05 for β_{13}). Therefore, full mediation through "size" exists (Baron and Kenny, 1986). In other words, mature MFIs grow in size and diversify into other products in addition to providing loans. The relationship between these three variables, as suggested by the results given in table 3, is shown in figure 3.

Figure 3. Relationship between age, size and providing only loans

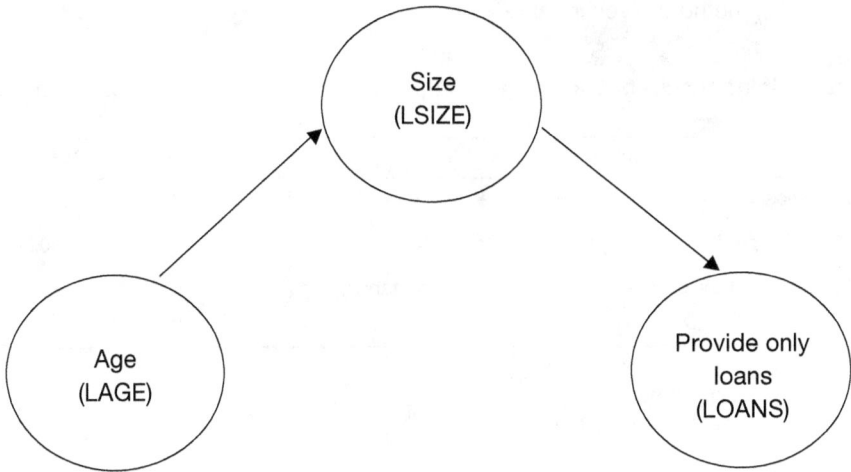

R_2 – *Relationship between age, emphasis on profitability and performance*

The relationship between age, emphasis on profitability and performance, as discussed in section III, under Testing for indirect and mediating effect, is shown in figure 4.

Figure 4. Relationship R2

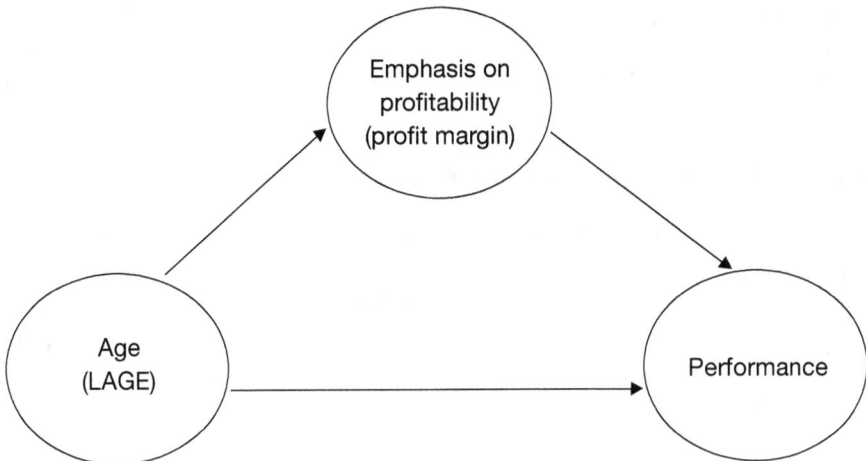

The results of the three regressions were run to test the mediating effect of "emphasis on profitability" between "age" and performance using the Baron and Kenny (1986) method, given in table 4.

Table 4. Relationship between age,[a] emphasis on profitability and performance

Regression models	β	Value of β_{ij}
Performance = $\beta_{01} + \beta_{11}$ Age + e_1	β_{11}	-0.08*
Emphasis on profitability = $\beta_{02} + \beta_{12}$ Age + e_2	β_{12}	0.24**
Performance = $\beta_{03} + \beta_{13}$ Age + β_{23} Emphasis on profitability + e_3	β_{13}	-0.12*
	β_{23}	0.30**

Notes: [a] Log transformations were used.

*$p < 0.05$, **$p < 0.01$.

Sample N = 234; cross-sectional data.

The first regression in table 4 shows that "age" has a significant negative effect on performance (*$p < 0.05$ and $\beta_{11} < 0$). This means that young MFIs perform better than older ones, which supports the hypothesis H_1, as shown earlier. The second regression shows that "age" has a significant positive impact on "emphasis on profitability" (**$p < 0.01$ and $\beta_{12} > 0$). This supports the argument discussed in section III, under Testing for indirect and mediating effect, that mature MFIs place greater emphasis on profitability.

In the third regression, when the mediating effect of "emphasis on profitability" is tested, "age" still has a significant negative effect on performance (*$p < 0.05$ and $\beta_{13} < 0$). Therefore, it can be concluded that any mediating effect of "emphasis on profitability" on the relationship between "age" and "performance" is insignificant, although there is a statistically significant relationship between age and emphasis on profitability.

Relevance of the main results to the Asia-Pacific region

The above analysis was repeated on the data relating to 70 MFIs in the sample that are located in the Asia-Pacific region. This was carried out to compare the relevance of the findings that were revealed in the main analysis to MFIs operating in the Asia-Pacific region. The Comparison of the results of Asia-Pacific countries analysis with those of the main sample covering all the countries are given in tables 5, 6, 7 and 8. The shaded columns relate to the results of the analysis conducted on MFIs in the Asia-Pacific region.

Table 5. Correlation matrix

Variables	Performance[1]	Performance[2]	Emphasis on profitability[1]	Emphasis on profitability[2]	Providing only loans[1]	Providing only loans[2]	Size[1]	Size[2]	Age[1]	Age[2]
1. Performance	1.00	1.00								
2. Emphasis on profitability	0.29**	0.37**	1.00	1.00						
3. Providing only loans	0.14*	-0.17++	-0.08	-0.21*	1.00	1.00				
4. Size[a]	-0.21	-0.17++	0.01	0.04	-0.23**	-0.13+	1.00	1.00		
5. Age[a]	-0.08*	-0.106	0.24**	0.14+	-0.16*	-0.24*	0.36**	0.47**	1.00	1.00

Notes: [a] Log transformations were used.

*p < 0.05, **p < 0.01 – significant relationships.

++ p < 0.07, +p < 0.13 – weak relationships.

[1] Sample size N = 234; cross-sectional data.

[2] Shaded columns relate to results of only Asia-Pacific countries; sample size N = 70; cross-sectional data.

Table 6. Regression results[a] of equation (1)

Independent variables	Unstan-dardized coefficient[1] (B)	Unstan-dardized coefficient[2] (B)	Standard error[1]	Standard error[2]	Standard-ized coefficient[1] (β)	Standard-ized coefficient[2] (β)
Emphasis on profitability	1.25	1.42	0.26	0.47	0.31**	0.35**
Providing only loans	0.31	-0.21	0.14	0.28	0.15*	-0.09
Size[b]	0.03	0.13	0.05	0.09	0.03	0.17
Age[b]	-0.18	-0.07	0.11	0.23	-0.11*	-0.04

Notes: [a] Dependent variable – performance.

   [b] Log transformations were used.

   * $p < 0.05$, **$p < 0.01$ – significant relationships.

   [1] Sample size $N = 234$; cross-sectional data.

   [2] Shaded columns relate to results of only Asia-Pacific countries; sample size $N = 70$; cross-sectional data.

Table7. Relationship between age,[a] size[a] and providing only loans

Regression models	β	Value of β_{ij}[1]	Value of β_{ij}[2]
Providing only loans = $\beta_{01} + \beta_{11}$ Age + e_1	β_{11}	-0.16**	-0.23*
Size = $\beta_{02} + \beta_{12}$ Age + e_2	β_{12}	0.36**	0.47**
Providing only loans = $\beta_{03} + \beta_{13}$ Age + β_{23} Size + e_3	β_{13}	-0.11	-0.22*
	β_{23}	-0.19**	-0.24

Notes: [a] Log transformations were used.

   * $p < 0.05$, **$p < 0.01$ – significant relationships.

   [1] Sample size $N = 234$; cross-sectional data.

   [2] Shaded columns relate to results of only Asia-Pacific countries; sample size $N = 70$; cross-sectional data.

Table 8. Relationship between age,[a] emphasis on profitability and performance

Regression models	β	Value of β_{ij} [1]	Value of β_{ij} [2]
Performance $= \beta_{01} + \beta_{11}$ Age $+ e_1$	β_{11}	-0.08*	0.11
Emphasis on profitability $= \beta_{02} + \beta_{12}$ Age $+ e_2$	β_{12}	0.24**	0.14++
Performance $= \beta_{03} + \beta_{13}$ Age $+ \beta_{23}$ emphasis on profitability $+ e_3$	β_{13}	-0.12*	0.06
	β_{23}	0.30**	0.36**

Notes:　[a] Log transformations were used.

　　　* $p < 0.05$, ** $p < 0.01$ – significant relationships.

　　　++ $p < 0.07$, + $p < 0.13$ – weak relationships.

　　　[1] Sample size N = 234; cross-sectional data.

　　　[2] Shaded columns relate to results of only Asia-Pacific countries; sample size N = 70; cross-sectional data.

The comparisons of results show that most of the findings in the main analysis are relevant to MFIs in the Asia-Pacific region. Some results show weak relationships between the variables ($p < 0.07$ and $p < 0.13$). This is due to the significant decrease in the sample size, which reduces the power and hence, the ability to pick up significant relationships. (Note that the sample size of 70 relating to the Asia-Pacific region is less than one third of the original sample size of 234). The conclusions that can be drawn from the relationships shown in the comparison tables can be summarized as follows.

Strong relationships ($p < 0.5$)

- MFIs grow in size with Age
- With age MFIs gain experience and go into product diversification
- Product diversification prompts MFIs to focus more on profits
- Emphasis on profits helps MFIs to perform better in alleviating poverty.

Weak relationships ($p < 0.13$)

- When MFIs grow in size, they go into product diversification ($p < 0.13$) and perform better in alleviating poverty compared to smaller MFIs ($p < 0.07$).
- Mature MFIs focus more on profits ($p < 0.13$).
- MFIs that go into product diversification perform better in alleviating poverty ($p < 0.07$).

It may be noted that there is one interesting change in the results when compared to those of the main sample. The Asia-Pacific sample shows that product diversification improves the performance while the main sample shows the opposite. This is a fact that can be argued from both sides. Obviously, the strong negative effect of the main sample may have overridden the positive effect in the small sample.

A detail discussion of the above results and the conclusions that can be drawn from the study are given in the next section.

V. DISCUSSION AND CONCLUSION

The main objective of this research was to study whether MFIs change their management policies with regard to emphasis on profitability and product diversification when they mature and expand in size, and whether such changes improve their performance with regard to poverty alleviation. This was done by analysing the relationships between five variables of MFIs that change over time: age; size; product diversification; emphasis on profitability; and performance, in relation to alleviation of poverty in a sustainable manner. An understanding of how product diversification and emphasis on profitability can affect the performance of MFIs in relation to alleviation of poverty in a sustainable manner is useful for managers of MFIs when setting organizational policies and also for the donors who *"may"* be influencing the policies of MFIs when they inject hundreds of millions of dollars into the microfinancing sector.

Data relating to 234 MFIs from 63 countries around the world, including countries in the Asia-Pacific region, were used in the study. The results of the main analysis conducted on these 234 MFIs given in section IV can be summarized and shown, as indicated in figure 5.

First, "age" (H_1), "providing only loans" or "not going into product diversification" (H_3) and "emphasis on profitability" (H_4) has a significant direct impact on the "performance" of MFIs in relation to alleviation of poverty (table 2 and figure 5).

The relationship between "age" and "performance" (H_1) is a negative one. This concurs with previous studies in other industries (Wagner 1995; Glancey 1998; Wijewardena and Tibbits, 1999; Almus and Nerlinger, 1999). Microfinancing is different from traditional banking and is a new industry that MFIs learn as they mature. Therefore, there is a tendency for newly established MFIs to learn from the mistakes made by mature ones. While the previous studies mentioned above were in different industries, the situation of microfinancing is probably similar to the post-Soviet Union companies of the Russian Federation that had to learn to operate in a market

Figure 5. Model showing all the significant relationships

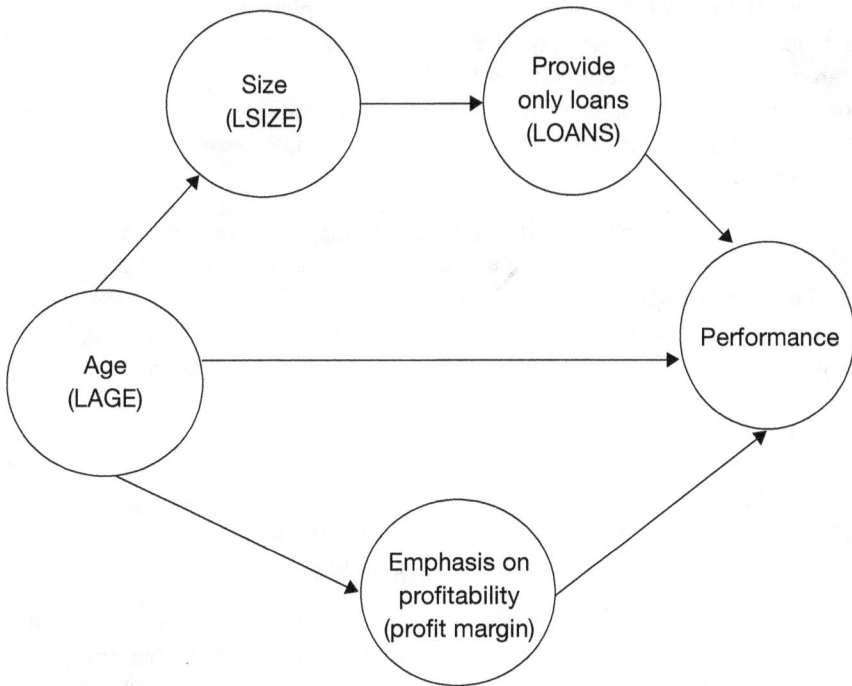

economy, which was completely new to them. Liuhto (2001), who studied the change in organizational performance of more than 1,000 post-Soviet Union companies found that *"younger organizational age is linked to positive change in performance"*.

The results also indicate that "emphasis on profitability" has a direct impact on "performance" (H_4). This result is not surprising because focusing on profits would encourage MFIs to be more efficient in their operations and also not to depend on subsidies from donors. The surpluses they make can be used to help more poor people, which improves their efforts to alleviate poverty. Therefore, the results of this study support those who argue for MFIs to take a "commercial approach" (Christen, 1998; Robinson, 1998; Schmidt and Zeitinger, 1994) against those that advocate a "welfare approach" (Marcus, Porter and Harper, 1999; CGAP, 2001).

The direct positive impact of "providing only loans" (not diversifying) on "performance" (H_3) is not expected. (However, this was not the case for MFIs in the Asia-Pacific countries, which is discussed later). In commercial companies, diversification provides stability and reduces the risk of relying on one product because every product has a limited life cycle. Therefore, it is expected that the diversified organizations will perform better, as argued by many scholars. However, as indicated by the results, this argument is not valid in microfinancing. The main reason for this is probably because of the large demand for microfinancing services compared to the supply (seller's market), which reduces the need for MFIs to diversify into other products or services for their survival. Offering loans to the poor without any security will be desired until global poverty is eliminated, which may take decades or even centuries.

Another contributing factor for this result may be that the gains from diversification, such as saving or insurance, could be far less compared with the costs. The savings deposit of the poor may be very small unlike in banks to yield an adequate return to cover administration costs, including costs of complying with regulations imposed by reserve banks and government authorities for taking deposits. This negative impact on the cash flow leaves fewer funds for MFIs to help more poor people, thus, reducing their performance in relation to poverty alleviation. Another reason may be that loan facilities are more important for the poor compared to savings facilities to improve their income levels. For example, attaining a loan is more difficult for the poor than having a place or a facility to save your money after earning it. However, further research is needed in this area to confirm this.

As shown in table 2, Hypothesis H_2 was not supported. "Size" did not have a direct impact on "performance" (H_2). Therefore, the results of this study support Gibrat's Law (1931) and challenge the findings of studies by Evans (1987), Hall (1987) and Almus and Nerlinger (1999), which found a significant and negative relationship between those two variables. It concurs with Audretsch and others, (2002), which found that Gibrat's Law is valid for the service industry. Microfinancing can be considered to be a type of service.

After analysing the direct impact of age, size, emphasis on profitability and providing only loans on the performance, the indirect and mediating effects among these variables were reviewed. Two relationships (R_1 and R_2 above) were analysed.

In R_1, the relationships between age, size and providing only loans were examined. Results show that age has a positive effect on the size (ref β_{12} in table 3), which is illustrated in figures 3 and 5. This was expected because the demand for microfinancing is much higher than the supply, as explained earlier. This means that over time. MFIs grow in size. This result supports the findings of other studies in which the average firm size increased with age (Hutchinson, Patrick and Walsh, 2010; Cabral and Mata, 2003).

It was also shown that age had a negative effect on "providing only loans" (ref β_{11} in table 3). This means that mature MFIs diversify into other products and services, such as savings accounts and insurance. This concurs with Farjourn (1994), Montgomery and Hariharan (1991), Chang (1996) and Ingram and Baum (1997), who argue that experience and knowledge gained due to age enhances the ability of organizations to diversify into other products. It was also found that "size" has a negative effect on "providing only loans" (ref β_{23} in table 3). In other words, when MFIs expand, they diversify into other products in addition to loans (product diversification). This is shown in figures 3 and 5 and is supported by previous studies done in other industries, namely Dass, 2000; Wheeler and others, 1999; Donaldson, 1982; Dawley, Hoffman and Brockman (2003); and Silverman and Castaldi, 1992. However, when the effect of size and age is controlled, there is no significant impact on "providing only loans" (note that β_{13} in table 3 is not significant). Therefore, the impact of "age" on "providing only loans" flows entirely through "size", which acts as a mediating variable between "age" and "providing only loans" (figures 3 and 5). The conclusion to be drawn here is that age and size have an impact on product diversification, similar to findings of other studies mentioned above. However, the effect of age on diversification in microfinancing is due to its influence on size.

In the last stage of the data analysis, the relationships between "age", "emphasis on profitability" and "performance" are reviewed (R_2). The results show a significant positive relationship between "age" and "emphasis on profitability" (β_{12} in table 4 and figure 5), which means that mature MFIs place greater emphasis on profits and take a commercial approach rather than a welfare approach. This supports the argument of Schmidt (2010) that most MFIs start as not-for-profit organizations and gradually convert to commercial enterprises. Some, such as Bancosol in Bolivia, have even gone to the extent of transforming into banks. This "mission drift" found in this study has been confirmed by case studies done in different countries (Drake and Rhyne, 2002; Rhyne, 2001; Sriram, 2010; Khan, 2010). One of the main reasons for mature MFIs to focus on profits could be the competition for limited donor funds and/or donor pressure, as explained by Epstein and Yuthas (2010). Thus, MFIs may be realizing the need to generate their own funds rather than rely on subsidies from donors.

Because both emphasis on profitability and age have significant direct impacts on performance (see table 2), and that age has a significant impact on emphasis on profitability (β_{12} in table 4) as shown in figure 4, the possible mediating effect of emphasis on profitability between age and performance was tested by using the Baron and Kenny (1986) method. The results shown in table 4 confirm that after controlling for the effects of emphasis on profitability, age has a significant impact on performance (β_{13} in table 4). This means that any mediating effect of emphasis on profitability on the relationship between age and performance is insignificant, although there is a statistically significant relationship between age and emphasis on profitability. The relationship between these three variables can be confirmed, as shown in figures 4 and 5.

Relevance of the findings to the Asia-Pacific region and policy implications

The analysis conducted on the 234 MFIs around the world was repeated on 70 MFIs in the sample located in the Asia-Pacific region. This was carried out mainly to compare and assess the applicability of the results of the main analysis to the Asia-Pacific region. The results and the analysis conducted on the Asia-Pacific region given in section IV, under Relevance of the main results to the Asia-Pacific region, indicate that the findings of the main study are applicable to the region. However, there is one exception. The main study indicates that product diversification has a negative effect on the performance in relation to alleviation of poverty, while the analysis on the sample of MFIs in the Asia-Pacific region shows this to be the complete opposite (positive effect). Therefore, smaller MFIs that focus on only providing loans (no product diversification) perform better than mature large MFIs in general, while in the Asia-Pacific region, the large mature MFIs that adopt product diversification perform better than those that only provide loans. The impact of product diversification on MFIs can be argued both ways as discussed earlier. The small size of savings deposits placed in MFIs, which makes them not financially viable, is believed to be the main reason for the negative impact. It may be that the savings deposits of MFIs in the Asia-Pacific region are generally larger compared to those in other parts of the world. The comparatively higher economic growth in some developing countries in the Asia-Pacific region may be one reason. However, further research is needed in this area.

Policy implications to MFIs in the Asia-Pacific region and the rest of the world related to the findings of this study is shown in figure 5. In conclusion, as MFIs mature, they tend to become larger. During this transformation, there is a shift in their management policies to adopt product diversification and focus more on profitability. These two changes have significant impacts on the performance of MFIs with regard to poverty alleviation. While emphasis on profitability has a positive effect on MFIs, the impact of product diversification depends on the region. In the Asia-Pacific region product diversification has had a positive impact on poverty alleviation. The mature large MFIs that adopt product diversification have performed better in alleviating poverty compared to those that have only focused on providing loans. In the other parts of the world, product diversification has had a negative impact on the performance with regard to poverty alleviation. Outside the Asia-Pacific region, young MFIs that have only focused on providing loans without product diversification have performed better than mature MFIs in alleviating poverty.

The findings of this study make a significant contribution to the existing knowledge in the microfinancing area. It improves the understanding of the transformations that MFIs go through over time in two key areas that contribute to their performance in relation to alleviation of poverty. No other empirical studies taking a global perspective (63 countries) or one that focuses on the Asia-Pacific region have been done previously in this area. Key lessons learned are that MFIs shift to focusing on profits and product diversification as they mature and expand in size. Emphasizing profitability improves the performance of MFIs in their poverty alleviation efforts. However, adopting product diversification has to be done with extreme caution after careful consideration. The results show that product diversification has a positive effect on the performance of MFIs in relation to alleviation of poverty in the Asia-Pacific region, but it has a strong negative impact in other parts of the world. These key lessons have significant policy implications for donors to and managers of MFIs that operate in countries in the Asia-Pacific region and in the rest of the world.

In addition to policy implications, the study also makes a contribution to academic research. It supports and challenges the results of previous studies on, for example, age, size and product diversification, in other industries compared to when applied to microfinancing. For example, this study reveals that Gibrat's Law (1931) is applicable to microfinancing. Gibrat's Law states that there is no relationship between firm size and performance.

Limitations and future research

There are a number of limitations to this study. First, it has not looked at the causes that have prompted MFIs to change their policies relating to the emphasis on profitability and product diversification. Donor pressure or lack of donor funding are possible causes. However, the study fails to include these variables in the model; it only confirms that as MFIs mature and expand in size, their policies towards these two key areas change.

Second, the data relate to a one-year period. The effect of some variables on others may have a time lag that exceeds a one-year period. Such impacts cannot be found in this study. Third, other than the factors considered in this study, there may be other variables that significantly affect the performance of MFIs. Examples of this in the type of empirical analysis used for this study are omitted variables, endogeneity and reverse causality may are examples of this. Therefore, future research can be carried out to improve this model with more variables that change over time using data that cover a number of years for longitudinal studies. The possible reasons for diversification to have a positive effect on the performance of MFIs in the Asia-Pacific region in contrast to the negative effect in other parts of the world is also another area that opens opportunities for future research. Although costs and size of the deposits are speculated as the cause, it needs to be further investigated.

Some of the MFIs in the sample may be adopting Islamic Microfinancing (IMFI) practices. However, in the data, this difference has not been identified or captured. IMFIs take a welfare approach and unlike conventional MFIs, they do not charge any interest for the loans granted to the poor. However, a service fee is charged to cover the operational costs without any profit. It may be interesting to compare the above relationships of IMFIs with those of the conventional MFIs. This is another area with immense potential for future research.

REFERENCES

Adams, Dale W. (1998). *Altruistic or Production Finance? A Donor's Dilemma.* Brookfield, Vermont, U.S.A: Ashgate Publishing.

Aitken, Rob (2010). Ambiguous incorporations: microfinance and global governmentality. *Global Networks*, vol. 10, No. 2, pp. 223-243.

Almus, Matthias, and Eric A. Nerlinger (1999). Growth of new technology based firms: which factors matter? *Small Business Economics,* vol. 13, No. 2, pp. 141-154.

Asian Development Bank (ADB) (2000). *Finance for the Poor: Microfinance Development Strategy.* Manila.

Audretsch, D.B., and others (2002). Gibrat's law, are the services different? *Review of Industrial Organization,* vol. 24, No. 3, pp. 301-324.

Baker, Douglas D., and John B. Cullen (1993). Administrative reorganisation and configurational context: the contingent effects of age, size, and change in size. *Academy of Management Journal*, vol. 36, No. 6, pp. 1251-1277.

Baron, Reuben M., and David A. Kenny (1986). The moderator-mediator variable distinction in social psychological research: conceptual, strategic, and statistical considerations. *Journal of Personality and Social Psychology*, vol. 51, No. 6, pp. 1173-1182.

Bateman, Milford (2010). *Why Doesn't Microfinance Work? The Destructive Rise of Local Neoliberalism.* London: Zed Books.

Bruck, Connie (2006). Millions for millions, *The New Yorker,* 30 October.

Cabral, Luis M.B., and Jose Mata (2003). On the evolution of the firm size distribution: facts and theory. *American Economic Review*, vol. 93, No. 4, pp. 1075-1090.

Chang, Seajin (1996). An evolutionary perspective on diversification and corporate restructuring. Entry, exit, and economic performance during 1981-89. *Strategic Management Journal*, vol. 17, No. 8, pp. 587-611.

Christen, Robert Peck (1998). Keys to financial sustainability. In *Strategic Issues in Microfinance.* Mwangi S. Kimenyi and others, eds. Brookfield, Vermont, U.S.A.: Ashgate Publishing.

Consultative Group to Assist the Poor (CGAP) (2001). Commercialisation and mission drift, the transformation of microfinance in Latin America. CGAP Occasional Paper, No. 5. Washington, D.C.: World Bank.

_____ (2002). Microfinance and the Millennium Development Goals. Donor Brief, No. 9. Washington, D.C.: World Bank.

_____ (2003). *Microfinance Consensus Guidelines: Definitions of Selected Financial Terms, Ratios, and Adjustments for Microfinance.* Washington, D.C.: World Bank.

Dass, Parshotam (2000). Relationship of firm size, initial diversification, and internationalization with strategic change. *Journal of Business Research*, vol. 48, No. 3, pp. 135-146.

Dawley, David D., James J. Hoffman, and Erich N. Brockman (2003). Do size and diversification type matter? An examination of post-bankruptcy outcomes. *Journal of Managerial Issues*, vol. 15, No. 4, pp. 413-429.

Donaldson, Lex (1982). Divisionalization and size: a theoretical and empirical critique. *Organization Studies*, vol. 3, No. 4, pp. 321-337.

Drake, Deborah, and Elisabeth Rhyne, eds. (2002). *The Commercialization of Microfinance: Balancing Business and Development*. Bloomfield, Connecticut, U.S.A.: Kumarian Press.

Dunford, Chrisopher (2001). Building better lives: sustainable integration of microfinance and education in health, family planning and HIV/AIDS prevention for the poorest entrepreneurs. *Journal of Microfinance*, vol. 3, No. 2, pp. 1-25.

Eikenberry, Angela M., and Jodie Draper Kluver (2004). The marketization of the nonprofit sector: civil society at risk? *Public Administration Review*, vol. 64, No. 2, pp.132-140.

Epstein, Marc J., and Kristi Yuthas (2010). Mission impossible: diffusion and drift in the microfinance industry. *Sustainability Accounting, Management and Policy Journal*, vol. 1, No. 2, pp. 201-221.

Evans, David S. (1987). Tests of alternative theories of firm growth. *Journal of Political Economy*, vol. 95, No. 4, pp. 657-674.

Farjourn, Moshe (1994). Beyond industry boundaries: human expertise, diversification and resource-related industry groups. *Organization Science*, vol. 5, No. 2, pp. 185-199.

Fernando, Jude L. (2006). Microcredit and empowerment of women: blurring the boundary between development and capitalism. In *Microfinance: Perils and Prospects,* Jude L. Fernando, ed. New York: Routledge Publishing.

Foundation for Development Corporation (1992). *Banking with the Poor; Case Studies Prepared by Leading Asian Banks and Non Governmental Organisations*. Brisbane, Australia.

Geiger, Scott W., and Luke H. Cashen (2007). Organizational size and CEO compensation: the moderating effect of diversification in downscoping organisations. *Journal of Managerial Issues*, vol. 19, No. 2, pp. 233-252.

Gibrat, R. (1931). *Les Inégalités Economiques.* Paris: Editionos Sirey. In French.

Glancey, Keith (1998*)*. Determinants of growth and profitability in small entrepreneurial firms. *International Journal of Entrepreneurial Behaviour & Research*, vol. 4, No. 1, pp. 18-27.

Hall, Browyn H. (1987). The relationship between firm size and firm growth in the US manufacturing sector. *Journal of Industrial Economics*, vol. 35, No. 4, pp. 583-606.

Hulme, David, and Paul Mosley (1996). *Finance Against Poverty.* London: Routledge Publishing.

Hutchinson, John, Jozef Konings Patrick, and Paul Walsh (2010). The firm size distribution and inter-industry diversification. *Review of Industrial Organization*, vol. 37, No. 2, pp. 65-82.

Ingram, Paul, and Joel A.C. Baum (1997). Opportunity and constraint: organizations' learning from the operating and competitive experience of industries. *Strategic Management Journal*, vol. 18, No. S1 (July), pp. 75-98.

Jiang, Fuxiu (2006). Determinants of diversification by listed firms in China. *Frontiers of Business Research in China*, vol. 2, No. 2, pp. 170-186.

Khan, Ashfaq Ahmad (2010). Commercialization of microfinance - Is the sector losing its identity by evading its original social service responsibility? *Social and Environmental Accountability Journal*, vol. 28, No. 2, pp. 78-90.

_____(2011). Dictating change, shouting success: Where is accountability? *Australasian Accounting, Business and Finance Journal*, vol. 5, No. 4, pp. 85-99.

Khandker, Shahidur, and Baqui Khalily (1996). The Bangladesh Rural Advancement Committee's Credit Programmes: performance and sustainability. Discussion Paper, No. 324. Washington, D.C.: World Bank.

Khandker, Shahidur R., Zahed Khan, and Baqui Khalily (1995). Sustainability of a government targeted credit program: evidence from Bangladesh. Discussion Paper, No. 316. Washington, D.C.: World Bank.

Liuhto, Karl (2001). How much does size, age, or industry membership matter in transition? Studying change in organizational behavior in almost 1,000 post-Soviet Companies. *Problems of Economic Transition*, vol. 43, No. 12, pp. 6-49.

Marcus, Rachel, Beth Porter, and Caroline Harper (1999). Money matters: understanding microfinance. Save the Children Working Paper, No. 19. London: Save the Children Foundation Press.

Mintzberg, Henry, and James Brian Quinn (1998). *Readings in the Strategy Process.* Upper Saddle River, New Jersey: Prentice Hall International.

Montgomery, Cynthia A., and S. Hariharan (1991). Diversified expansion by large established firms. *Journal of Economic Behavior and Organization*, vol. 15, No. 1, pp. 71-87.

Mort, Gillian Sullivan, Jay Weerawardena, and Kashonia Carnegie (2003). Social entrepreneurship; towards conceptualization. *International Journal of Nonprofit and Voluntary Sector Marketing,* vol. 8, No 1, pp. 76-88.

Nanayakkara, Gemunu (2012). Measuring the performance of microfinancing institutions; a new approach. *South Asia Economic Journal,* vol. 13, No. 1, pp. 89-104.

Owens, John V. and Sylvia B. Wisniwiski (1999). Microsavings: what we can learn from informal savings. Presentation. Available from www.wiwi.uni-frankfurt.de/finance/schmidt/ndf/ndf_3/thu_rural_owens_wisniwski_pres.pdf.

Piergiovanni, Roberta, and others (2002). Gibrat's law and the firm size/firm growth relationship in Italian services. Timbergen Institute Discussion Paper. Rome: Department of National Accounts & Statistics of Italy.

Pitt, Mark, and Shahidur R. Khandker (1996). Household and intra-household impact of the Grameen Bank and similar targeted credit programs in Bangladesh. Discussion Paper, No. 320. Washington, D.C.: World Bank.

Reed, Larry, and Jan Maes (2012). *State of the Microcredit Summit Campaign Report 2012.* Available from www.microcreditsummit.org/resource/46/state-of-the-microcredit-summit.html.

Rhyne, Elisabeth (2001). *Mainstreaming Microfinance: How Lending to the Poor Began, Grew and Came of Age in Bolivia*. Boulder, Colorado, U.S.A.: Kumarian Press.

Robinson, M. (1998). *Microfinance: the Paradigm Shift from Credit Delivery to Sustainable Financial Intermediation.* Brookfield, Vermont, U.S.A.: Ashgate Publishing.

Robinson, Marguerite S. (2001). *The Microfinance Revolution: Sustainable Finance for the Poor.* Washington, D.C.: World Bank.

_____(2002). *The Microfinance Revolution,* vol. 2, *Lessons from Indonesia.* Washington, D.C.: World Bank.

Rogaly, Ben (1996). Microfinance evangelism, 'destitute women', and the hard selling of a new anti-poverty formula. *Development in Practice*, vol. 6, No. 2, pp. 100-112.

Schmidt, Reinhard H. (2010). Microfinance commercialization and ethics. *Poverty and Public Policy,* vol. 2, No. 1, pp. 99-137.

Schmidt, Reinhard H., and Claus-Peter Zeitinger (1994). *Critical Issues in Micro-business Finance and the Role of Donors.* In *Strategic Issues in Microfinance.* Mwangi S. Kimenyi and others, eds. Brookfield, Vermont, U.S.A.: Ashgate Publishing. Burlington: Ashgate Publishing.

Silverman, Murray, and Richard M. Castaldi (1992). Antecedents and propensity for diversification: a focus on small banks. *Journal of Small Business Management*, vol. 30, No. 2, pp. 42-52.

Sriram, M.S. (2010). Commercialisation of microfinance in India: a discussion on the emperor's apparel. *Economic and Political Weekly*, vol. 45, No. 24, pp. 65-73.

Valenzuela, Liza (2002). Getting the recipe right, the commercialisation of microfinance. In *The Commercialization of Microfinance: Balancing Business and Development,* Deborah Drake and Elisabeth Ryne, eds. Boulder, Colorado, U.S.A.: Kumarian Press.

Vogel, Robert C. (1984). Savings mobilization: the forgotten half of rural finance. In *Undermining Rural Development with Cheap Credit,* Douglas Graham and Dale W. Evans, eds. Boulder, Colorado, U.S.A.: Westview Press.

_____(1998). *Other People's Money: Regulatory Issues Facing Microenterprise Finance Programs.* Washington, D.C.: Communications Corporation.

Wagner, Joachim (1995). Exports, firm size, and firm dynamics. *Small Business Economics,* vol. 7, No. 1, pp. 29-39.

Wheeler, J.R.C., and others (1999). Financial and organisational determinants of hospital diversification into subacute care. *Health Services Research*, vol. 34, No. 1, pp. 61-81.

Wijewardena, Herma, and Garry E. Tibbits (1999). Factors contributing to the growth of small manufacturing firms: data from Australia. *Journal of Small Business Management*, vol. 37, No. 2, pp. 88-96.

World Bank (2009). *The World Bangkok Annual Report 2009: the Year in Review.* Washington, D.C.

Yaron, Jacob (1992). Assessing development finance institutions. A public interest analysis. Policy Research Working Paper, No. 174. Washington, D.C.: World Bank.

Yasuda, Takihido (2005). Firm growth, size, age and behavior in Japanese manufacturing. *Small Business Economics*, vol. 24, No. 1, pp. 1-15.

Yunus, Muhammad, and Alan Jolis (2001). *Banker to the Poor: the Autobiography of Muhammad Yunus.* New York: Oxford University Press.

FOOD PRICES AND THE DEVELOPMENT OF MANUFACTURING IN INDIA

Richard Grabowski*

Structural change associated with rapid growth has not occurred in labour-intensive manufacturing in India. It is argued in the present paper that this is at least partly due to the rise in the relative cost of labour, which is the result of the rising cost of food stemming from rapid overall growth and sluggish growth in agricultural productivity. A theoretical model has been developed and the experience of India is used to illustrate the model and its implications.

JEL classification: O1, O5, Q1.

Keywords: India, food prices, manufacturing.

I. INTRODUCTION

Economic growth over extended periods of time tends to be accompanied by dramatic structural change. Initially, poor countries are dominated by the agricultural sector. This sector makes up a large proportion of gross domestic product (GDP) and employment. Rapid growth in GDP is usually accompanied by a decline in the share of agriculture in GDP and employment. The fall in the share of agriculture in GDP generally declines more rapidly than the share of agriculture in total employment, but as employment in modern manufacturing and services rapidly grows, labour in the agricultural sector gravitates to the manufacturing and services sectors at a quick pace. This is because manufacturing is initially labour intensive in nature. Ultimately, the service sector becomes the dominant economic activity as modern services replace traditional, labour-intensive services and manufacturing. Of course, the growth process does not necessarily unfold in such a manner. Initial conditions, such as the relative abundance of land, may have a significant influence on the type of structural change that takes place (Dorin, Hourcade and Benoit-Cattin, 2013).

_____

*   Department of Economics, Southern Illinois University, Carbondale, Illinois 62901 (e-mail: ricardo@
siu.edu).

Recently, this structural change process has seemingly gone awry and the feasibility of this path of economic development has been called into question. Consequently, it may no longer be possible for a country to utilize rapid growth in manufacturing to absorb labour from agriculture and provide productive employment without significant policy changes. Rodrik (2014) has shown that manufacturing as a share of GDP and employment in many developing countries is failing to achieve the levels attained by East and South-East Asia during their periods of rapid growth and structural change. More specifically, in many developing countries, manufacturing as a share of GDP and employment appears to be declining, which is raising fears of a deindustrialization process.

This is important for a number of reasons. If rapid growth is achieved without rapid expansion in labour-intensive activities, such as manufacturing, how will this labour be productively incorporated into the economy? In addition, much of the early growth in poor countries comes from shifting labour from agriculture, where labour productivity is low, to manufacturing where labour productivity is much higher. This is a comparative static gain from shifting labour from one sector to another. Furthermore, there is a dynamic gain from this shift, which has been documented by Rodrik (2013), who has shown that unconditional convergence in labour productivity tends to occur in manufacturing. That is, once a manufacturing sector is firmly established in a less developed region, labour productivity in that sector tends to converge to that found in that same sector in developed countries. Thus, aggregate (economy-wide) convergence generally fails to occur in many low income countries because manufacturing remains too small of a share in the overall economy. Therefore, there is a dynamic gain and a comparative static gain in labour productivity that results from shifting labour. These gains will be lost if the structural change breaks down.

India also has experienced a structural change process that is quite different from the experiences in East and South-East Asia and the currently developed countries. In the case of India, economic growth has been characterized by the rapid expansion of modern sector services. Manufacturing, especially labour-intensive manufacturing, has failed to grow rapidly. In addition, the existing modern industrial sector has become increasingly capital intensive in nature (Kochhar and others, 2006). Direct employment in agricultural production has declined, but much of the labour, which had worked in agriculture, is involved in rural, non-farm, informal economic activities. Some scholars have labelled this as "stunted structural transformation" (Binswanger-Mkhize, Peter and D'Sousa, 2011).

Therefore, how can the lack of development of labour-intensive manufacturing in today's developing countries be explained? One set of arguments emphasizes the changes in technology that have occurred. This change in technology allows for the production of a good to be broken into pieces, which are located in various parts of the world, resulting in less development of manufacturing in any particular place (Baldwin, 2011). Labour-intensive technologies are also being replaced with those requiring less labour. Even for those manufactured goods that have been characterized as labour intensive, technical innovation seems to be capital intensive in nature (Felipe, Mehta and Rhee, 2014). In addition, in many places in the world, government regulations have made physically abundant labour economically expensive to use. This has made it very difficult for labour-intensive manufacturing to expand. All of these factors have certainly played a role, but in the present paper, an additional explanation is developed, which is based on the cost of food.

The argument is fairly straightforward. A three-sector model composed of food producing agriculture, services, and manufacturing is developed. The service sector is closed to trade, while manufacturing and agriculture are open to trade. An exogenous increase in food prices is allowed to occur. An implication of the model is that labour will flow into agriculture and out of manufacturing while the service sector will maintain its share of labour. As a result, manufacturing will decline or, in other words, deindustrialization will occur.

A second version of the model is developed in which the service and manufacturing sectors are assumed to be human capital intensive (modern) and open to trade. The food production sector is also open, but the large country case is assumed. An exogenous external increase in the demand for modern services will lead to a rise is the relative price of food. As a result, once again the manufacturing sector will decline.

The models are then applied to the experience of India. A discussion of the trend in manufacturing and structural change is presented. Data on food inflation and real wages are examined. The conclusion drawn indicates that increases in the price of food have made labour more expensive, making it difficult to develop a comparative advantage in labour-intensive manufacturing.

This paper unfolds as follows. In the second section, the theoretical basis of the paper is developed. Section III applies the model to the experience of India. Finally, section IV contains a summary of the paper and a discussion of policy implications.

II. SOME THEORETICAL ANALYSIS

Much of classical economics and modern dualistic economic analysis has been concerned with agriculture, the price of food and structural change. Ricardo (1965) has focused heavily on the operation of the law of diminishing returns in agriculture and how that would affect the growth of manufacturing. Lowering corn prices through the elimination of the Corn Laws was seen as a mechanism for promoting prosperity in England. Although without technical innovation, such prosperity might have been short-lived.

Dualistic models based on the classical perspective also tend to place importance on the role of food in the process of economic development. In the model of dualistic economic development developed by W. Arthur Lewis, the economy is divided into modern and traditional sectors. The modern sector uses capital and labour, saved and accumulated capital and maximized profit. Although Lewis argued that this sector is composed of many different types of products, others have generally identified it with manufacturing (Lewis, 1954). The traditional sector, which is often identified with agriculture, especially food production, utilizes land and labour, engages in no savings, is characterized by output sharing rather than profit maximizing, and is burdened with surplus labour. Assuming a closed model with no technological innovation, growth occurs as the result of the shift of labour from agriculture, in which the marginal product of labour is zero or very low as compared to the manufacturing sector which has greater labour productivity. As a result, growth comes from structural change.

As long as surplus labour exists, food problems do not arise. However, once it is exhausted, food production declines, which puts upward pressure on real wages in the modern manufacturing sector. This, in turn, threatens the expansion of manufacturing and thus the source of growth and structural change may likely be inhibited. Consequently, in this type of model a sort of balanced growth process is needed. Most importantly, productivity in agriculture, in particular food staples, is the key to enabling the structural change process to unfold. There are many criticisms one can make of this sort of analysis. The meaning of the concept of surplus labour has been debated heavily and doubt has been cast on its empirical validity. In addition, the model, as outlined, is closed in nature. If the model economy is opened to trade and assuming a small country case, the situation changes. Saving and investment in manufacturing result in a shift of labour (structural change), but food prices are fixed by imports. If a comparative advantage in manufacturing is developed, then exports from this sector can be used to finance the imports of food. Under this scenario, structural change can successfully occur as food loses its importance in the development story.

Models can be developed in a way that would not be subject to those criticisms and allow the production of food staples to continue to play a critical role in the process of structural change. The series of models explained here are based on the work of Gollin, Jedwab and Vollrath (2013). The first model to be discussed is of a three sector economy: agriculture (staple food production), labour-intensive manufacturing, and services, which are also assumed to be labour intensive in nature. The latter is a traditional service sector, which is labour intensive and produces services on a small scale (not modern sector services, such as banking and finance). The economy is open to international trade in terms of manufacturing and food staples, but closed in terms of the service sector. It is assumed that these types of services are non-tradable.

Although the staple food sector is open to trade, the large country case is being assumed. That is, increased purchases or sales of food can influence the domestic price of food. This assumption is made because India is indeed a large country, geographically and in terms of population. In addition, the international markets for most food staples are very thin in nature. Trade in most food staples is relatively limited because few developing nations wish to rely on imports to meet a significant part of their food needs. In 2000, almost 70 per cent of the arable land in developing countries was devoted to food staples (grains, pulses, roots and tubers). Of this production, almost all of it was devoted to domestic consumption. Few developing nations are exporters of grain. For example, Argentina has been exporting more than a quarter of its grain crop (Gollin, Parentz and Rogerson, 2007) while Brazil has become a major exporter of corn. As a result, international markets are thin and changes in purchases by any large economy are likely to have dramatic effects on the domestic prices of particular food staples.

The manufacturing (labour-intensive) sector is also assumed to be open to trade, but the small country case is assumed here and prices are, therefore, exogenous. It is initially assumed that the country has a comparative disadvantage in food and thus is an importer. Alternatively, the country is also assumed to have a comparative advantage in labour-intensive manufacturing, that is, the country is relatively labour abundant. Of course, even countries that are labour abundant do not automatically have a comparative advantage in labour-intensive manufacturing. Infrastructure must be provided, market failures must be compensated for and coordination problems must be solved. Thus, the state plays a critical role in the development of this comparative advantage.

Food-producing agriculture is assumed to utilize land and labour in the production process. Manufacturing and services both use only labour. However, the former provides a tradable good and the latter a non-tradable good.

In this context, when assuming an exogenous increase in the relative price of food, there is a large shock in terms of prices. This, in turn, results in the expansion of domestic food production which would require increased amounts of labour. This labour cannot come from the service sector as its output is non-tradable and the labour associated with it must remain in that sector in order to produce the same level of services. Actual service production may need to expand as these traditional services are usually associated with the production and processing of food. Real wages in food production and possibly the traditional service sector will rise and labour will be drawn from the manufacturing sector with production in that sector declining. This basically involves the undermining of the developing country's comparative advantage in labour-intensive manufacturing. One might call this a process of deindustrialization as the capability to produce labour-intensive manufacturing has declined.

A variation on the above model can be developed by adding a modern service sector, which utilizes only human capital as an input in the production process while subsuming the traditional service sector into the food production sector. It is assumed that the country has a comparative advantage in modern sector services, a potential comparative advantage in manufacturing, and a comparative disadvantage in food production.

In this context, a dramatic rise in external demand for modern sector services will have a number of effects. In particular, production and income in this sector will rise. Increased income is presumed to be spent on food, manufactured goods, and traditional services. Thus, the food and traditional services sectors will require additional labour to expand production. This labour will have to be drawn from the manufacturing sector, as the increased demand for this sector's output will be met by imports. This will be accomplished through a rise in the relative price of food and in real wages in this sector relative to manufacturing. This will likely undermine the potential comparative advantage that manufacturing has and thus result in deindustrialization, in the sense of reduced capability to produce.

It should be pointed out that the rising wages discussed above are likely, in the long run, to lead to an increase in mechanization of the production process in agriculture. As a result, employment opportunities are likely to grow slowly in that sector in the long term. Consequently, much of the expansion in employment will likely be in traditional services.

In the two scenarios outlined above, the price of food plays a critical role in the analysis. Rising food prices resulting from an exogenous shock or as the result of the rapid expansion of another sector of the economy (modern services) draws resources away from and undermines the comparative advantage in manufacturing. Rapid productivity growth in the food sector, which leads to a reduction in the relative price of food and real wage costs in manufacturing, makes maintaining or developing a comparative advantage in manufacturing more likely.

In the next section of the paper, this analysis is illustrated through the experiences of India during the period since the emergence of higher growth rates. The discussion shows that labour intensity in manufacturing in India has declined, partly as a result of rising real wages associated with an increase in the relative price of food.

III. AN INDIAN EXAMPLE

Beginning in the 1980s, India has been experiencing a period of relatively rapid economic growth, which represents a dramatic change from the past. As a result, structural change has indeed occurred in the economy. The share of agricultural production in GDP fell from 41.1 per cent in 1972-1973 to 14.1 per cent in 2011-2012. This has also been matched by a decline in the share of employment in agricultural activities from 73.9 per cent in 1972-1973 to 48.9 per cent in 2011-2012 (Reddy, 2015). This is just what one would expect to occur as the growth and development process unfold.

However, the decline in the proportion of labour employed in agriculture has not been accompanied by an increase in manufacturing as a share of either total employment or production. This contradicts the process of structural change followed by countries in East Asia and South-East Asia. In those countries, the relative contraction in agriculture as a share of production and employment was accompanied by a rise in manufacturing as a share of production and employment (as well as a rise in modern sector services). The result of this process of structural change has been rapid growth in employment opportunities outside of agriculture. The case of the Republic of Korea is a good example of this process (Amirapu and Subramanian, 2015).

The concern for India is that growth that bypasses labour-intensive manufacturing is likely to be growth that generates only a slow increase in employment opportunities. The view that manufacturing has failed to play the usual role in the development process is supported by the work of Amirapu and Subramanian (2015).

Data on labour productivity in the Indian economy, excluding agriculture, are presented in table 1. As indicated, labour productivity in registered manufacturing has been quite high, only exceeded by that in modern services. Thus, the potential for rapid growth in labour productivity through the shift in resources from agriculture to modern manufacturing and services certainly exists in India.

Table 1. Growth of labour productivity in India (%)

Sector	1984-2010	2000-2010
Aggregate economy	3.7	4.0
Non-manufacturing	3.7	3.9
Services	4.9	6.3
Manufacturing	3.7	4.2
Registered manufacturing	4.4	5.4
Unregistered manufacturing	2.2	1.2

Source: Adapted from Amirapu and Subramanian (2015).

However, data reveal that India has not been able to adequately take advantage of the opportunity with respect to manufacturing. Tables 2 and 3 show the share of registered (modern) manufacturing in total employment and in total production. As indicated, the share in terms of employment has actually declined whereas the share in terms of output has increased very little.

The most abundant factor of production in India has been unskilled labour. Only a slim majority of those employed in India have attained a primary level education, while only 20 per cent of workers have had a secondary education. With this skill base, one would expect that the most dynamic sector would likely be labour-intensive manufacturing. In the previous paragraphs, it was shown that modern manufacturing growth has been relatively slow and that the increase in manufacturing that has occurred required skilled labour (Kochhar and others, 2006). The registered

Table 2. Growth in employment shares

Sector	1984	2010	Annual growth (1984-2010)
Registered manufacturing	.027	.026	-0.2%
Aggregate services	.201	.219	0.3%
Trade, hotel, etc.	.074	.093	0.9%
Communications	.028	.038	1.2%
Financial services and insurance	.006	.007	0.7%
Real estate, business services	.002	.011	7.1%
Construction	.031	.080	3.7%

Source: Adapted from Amirapu and Subramanian (2015).

Table 3. Growth in output shares

Sector	1984	2010	Annual growth (1984-2010)
Registered manufacturing	.091	.195	0.6%
Aggregate services	.358	.528	1.5%
Trade, hotel, etc.	.120	.152	0.9%
Communications	.056	.075	1.1%
Financial services and insurance	.035	.058	2.0%
Real estate, business services	.053	.108	2.81%
Construction	.056	.087	1.7%

Source: Adapted from Amirapu and Subramanian (2015).

manufacturing sector is indeed skilled-labour intensive (Amirapu and Subramanian, 2015).

Sen and Das (2014) provide further evidence that the labour intensity of Indian production, in particular manufacturing, has been declining. Evidence of this is given by calculating the output elasticity of employment. From 1990 to 2000, value added in manufacturing grew by 6.7 per cent per year, while employment growth was 1.81 per cent, resulting in an employment elasticity of output of 0.27. However, from 2000 to 2010 the output elasticity of employment fell to 0.05.

Sen and Das (2014) calculated the labour to fixed capital ratio for the entire three digit organized manufacturing sector for every year (and for each industry) for the period 1980-1981 to 2009-2010. The average labour intensity ratio for the organized manufacturing sector as a whole was 0.84. Industries, with ratios above this were classified as labour intensive while those with ratios below this were classified as capital intensive. Sen and Das (2014) show, using this information, that from the 1980s to 2010, labour intensity across fifty-two National Industrial Classification (NIC) three digit sectors fell from 1.45 to 0.33. The pace of decline was the highest for the most labour-intensive sectors (Sen and Das, 2014).

The immediate question that comes to mind is why this has occurred in India. This is in complete contrast to the experiences of East Asia, China, and Viet Nam. Some have argued that this is the result of strict labour laws in the country governing the conditions of employment, which significantly increase the cost of hiring labour. This would induce firms to substitute capital for labour. However, Sen and Das (2014) point out that while this argument relates to the level of capital and labour intensity, it fails to provide an explanation for the decline of labour intensity over time as this would require a scenario in which labour laws were to become increasingly inflexible (which does not seem to be the case). They propose an alternative explanation in which the declining labour intensity of production is attributed to a rise in the wage to rental price of capital ratio. Labour has become relatively more expensive or, an alternative way of expressing it, capital has become increasingly cheap. This is why manufacturing has become more capital intensive (less labour intensive).

They calculate the rental rate of capital as follows:

$$R_{it} = (PK_t (r_t - \pi_t))/P_{it} \tag{1}$$

Where PK_t is the price of capital goods in year t, P is the output price level of industry i at time t, r is the nominal bank lending rate at time t, and π is the rate of inflation. As shown in figure 1, the ratio of average wage to rental price of capital rises for both registered manufacturing as a whole (All-w/r) and for labour-intensive manufacturing (LI-w/r). The ratio rises slowly until mid-1990 and then rises more rapidly after that with the ratio for labour-intensive industry increasing faster.

Figure 1. Ratio of wage to rental price of capital

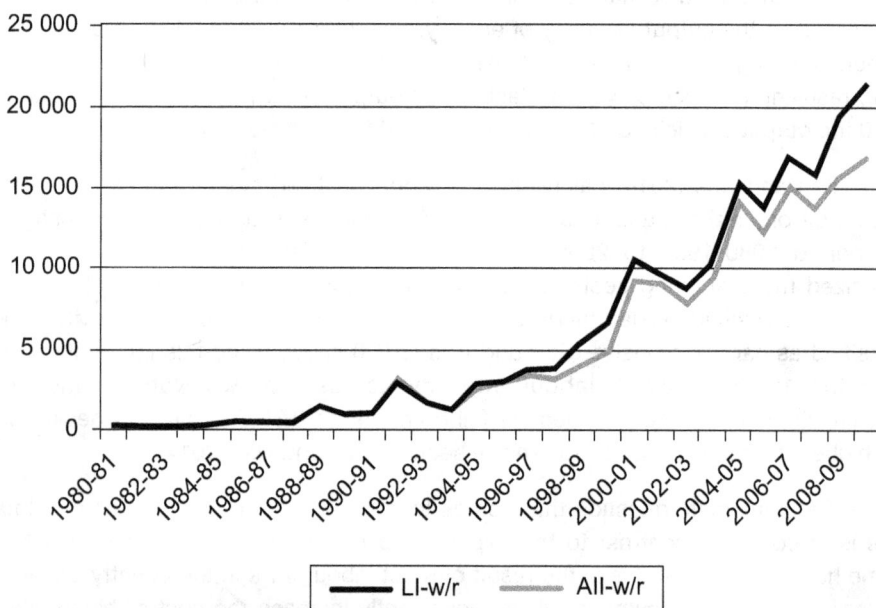

Source: Sen and Das (2014).

Notes: LI-w/r, wage to rental rate for labour-intensive industry; All-w/r, wage to rental rate for manufacturing as a whole.

Now the interesting thing about these results concerns what it is driving the change in the ratio. It seems that real wages in manufacturing are rising while the rental price of capital is falling. Thus, the rise in the ratio is due to a rise in real wages and a fall in the rental price of capital. The latter began to decline in the early 1990s, while the former rose throughout the period (1980-2010) (Sen and Das, 2014). Figure 2 illustrates the rise in real wages.

Figure 2. Real wage to rental rate for manufacturing as a whole

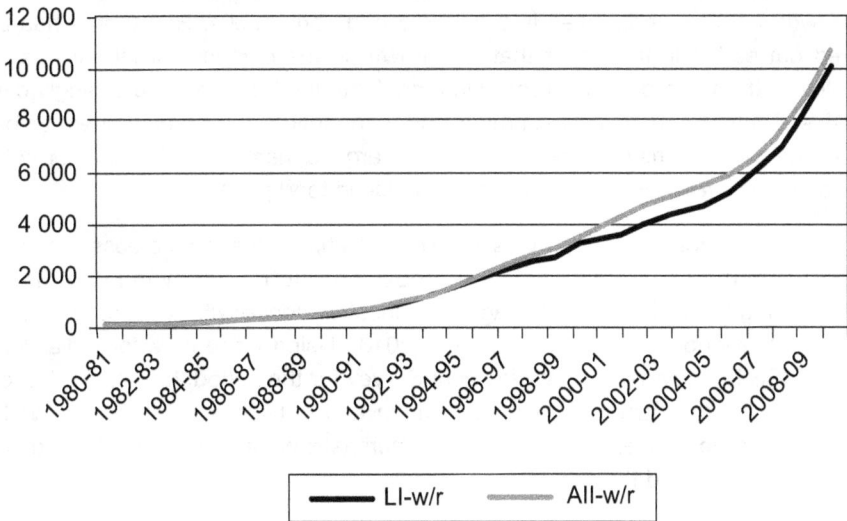

Source: Sen and Das (2014).

Notes: LI-w/r, wage to rental rate for labour-intensive industry; All-w/r, wage to rental rate for manufacturing as a whole.

Sen and Das (2014) attribute the fall in the rental price of capital to economic reforms undertaken in the early 1990s. The reforms led to a reduction in the nominal rate of protection for a variety of different types of capital goods. With declining protection, Indian firms could take advantage of the cheap capital goods available in international markets. This is related to arguments made earlier in this paper concerning factors that account for the lack of development of labour-intensive manufacturing. Specifically, technical innovation, which has enabled greater automation of even labour-intensive production processes, combined with a globalization process that has unbundled the manufacturing production process, has resulted in increased capital intensity and a dispersal of the supply chain in manufacturing. The analysis of Sen and Das (2014) supports this point of view.

The focus of this paper is on the rise in the real wage rate in India. In the previous paragraph, the rising wage in manufacturing was discussed. However, it appears that real wages in agriculture, in particular farming, have also been increasing. In particular, from 1990-1991 to 2000-2001, the real wage rate rose at an annual rate of 3.7 per cent. From 2001 to 2002, the real wage rose at an annual rate of 2.1 per cent. However, from 2006 to 2007, the rate accelerated dramatically (Wiggins and Keats, 2014). In summary, the real wage rose in both the agriculture and manufacturing sectors. From this, the key question is what is driving this rise in real wages? One could speculate that the rise is the result of rapid economic growth that began with reforms undertaken in the 1980s and early 1990s. However, it has been pointed out earlier in the paper that the growth in the demand for labour has been very slow with the production process in manufacturing becoming increasingly capital intensive. Therefore, demand stemming from economic growth would seem to be an unlikely cause of a rise in real wages. It is argued here that at least part of the increase in real wages is the result of an increase in food prices.

In the previous section, it was shown theoretically that an increase in the price of food stimulates an expansion in food production, drawing labour from manufacturing by raising the real wage. Empirical evidence with respect to this issue in India is provided in the work of Jacoby (2013). Using wage data for India derived from the NSS Employment-Unemployment Survey for the period 2004-2009, he found that real wages for manual labour both within and outside agriculture rose with an increase in food producer prices. The wage increases were most rapid in the districts where prices increased the most.

There is evidence indicating that this relationship also holds in other places. Van Campenhout, Pauw and Minot (2013) have utilized data drawn from Uganda. They have found that in the short run a rise in food prices has a negative effect on household welfare. However, in the long run, the welfare levels of rural households rise sharply because of increased returns to household labour and farm land coupled with an increase in the prices of food commodities sold. Wiggins and Keats (2014) have found that this has been the case throughout much of Asia.

Farm prices, in particular the price of food, have increased over time in India. Table 4 presents data on the wholesale price index for all commodities (WPIAC), the wholesale price index for all agricultural items (WPIFA), and the consumer price index for industrial worker-food (CPIIWF). As indicated, not only did the last two indices (measuring agricultural and food price changes, respectively) increase over time, but they also rose more rapidly than the overall price index.

Table 4. Price indices for India

Year	WPIAC	WPIFA	CPIIWF
1982	100.00	100.00	100.00
1983	104.90	111.00	102.30
1984	112.80	127.00	117.60
1985	120.10	132.00	122.00
1986	125.40	134.00	128.00
1987	132.70	148.00	141.00
1988	143.50	161.00	152.00
1989	154.20	177.00	169.00
1990	165.70	179.00	177.00
1991	182.70	201.00	199.00
1992	207.80	241.00	230.00
1993	228.70	271.00	254.00
1994	247.80	284.00	272.00
1995	276.64	320.92	304.00
1996	298.87	346.48	337.00
1997	313.69	389.08	369.00
1998	326.04	400.44	388.20
1999	345.80	451.56	445.00
2000	358.15	471.44	446.00
2001	382.85	485.64	453.00
2002	397.67	499.84	466.00
2003	410.02	508.36	477.00
2004	432.25	516.88	495.00
2005	461.89	528.24	506.00
2006	479.44	554.40	527.00
2007	511.71	612.48	575.00
2008	535.76	654.72	620.63
2009	580.86	712.80	698.21
2010	599.30	818.40	803.17
2011	659.23	950.40	885.32
2012	719.16	1 019.04	940.08

Source: Adapted from Sasmal (2015).

What was the cause of the rising relative price of food in India over the last several decades? From the 1980s onward, the rate of growth in GDP per capita has increased substantially. In addition, periods of negative annual growth have been relatively rare. Although Engel's law predicts that as the standard of living rises, households spend a smaller share of their budgets on food and food-related items, food remains a significant allocation in most family budgets in India. Thus, more rapid economic growth is likely to lead to rapid growth in the demand for food and related items. If domestic production fails to keep up and India represents a large country case, then indeed one would expect that food prices will be driven upward.

Sasmal (2015) utilizes time series data and the Granger causality analysis to determine whether growth in economic output per capita as measured by net national product per capita causes food prices increases. He utilizes data on the growth in the production of food grains, per capita net national product, expenditures by central and state governments, money supply, and changes in the exchange rate between the Indian rupee relative to the US dollar. The results of the analysis show that growth in net national product per capita significantly explains much of the food price inflation in India. The increase in real wages in both the agriculture and non-agriculture sectors stemming from rising food prices has played a role in making labour relatively more expansive than capital. This, in turn, has led to a reduction in the labour intensity of production processes, especially in manufacturing and particularly in labour-intensive manufacturing.

However, several other factors supporting the rising relative cost of food must be noted. Although expenditures on food have increased significantly as economic growth has occurred, the composition of those expenditures has begun to change. A greater share of expenditures is devoted to protein-rich foods and fruits and vegetables, while expenditures on food grains as a share of household budgets has begun to decline. Production of the former products has failed to keep pace with demand, which has increasingly made them the source of rising food prices (Bhattacharya, Rao and Gupta, 2014)

The problems involved with shifts in demand (sluggish supply response for, among others, fruits, vegetables and meat) are compounded by the minimum price support policies set by the government. These types of programmes are mainly aimed at food grains, such as rice, wheat, coarse cereals, and pulses. Table 5 shows the growth rate of minimum price supports compared to the growth of the wholesale price index for two different time periods. As indicated, minimum support prices began to rise at a very rapid rate during the period 2006-2012. This in itself tended to add to the rising food prices, in particular, those associated with rice, wheat, coarse cereals, and pulses.

Table 5. Growth of minimum support prices and wholesale prices

Commodity		Average annual growth rate (%)	
		2001-2002 to 2006-2007	2007-2008 to 2012-2013
Rice	MSP	3.52	10.90
	WPI	1.21	9.40
Wheat	MSP	2.46	9.69
	WPI	3.55	6.66
Coarse cereals	MSP	2.18	15.35
	WPI	5.49	11.22
Pulses	MSP	3.04	16.37
	WPI	6.68	8.49

Source: Adapted from Bhattacharya, Rao and Gupta (2014).

Notes: MSP, minimum support price; WPI, wholesale price index.

An indirect effect of higher support prices has also occurred. Specifically, products subject to minimum price supports distort the allocation of resources among various food products. That is, the major food grains receive a support price whereas other agricultural products do not. This raises the relative price of the former relative to the latter and, consequently, causes resources to flow towards grain production and away from fruits and vegetables, among other products. Therefore, as income has grown in India, the demand for fruits, vegetables and meat has risen dramatically (relative to grains), while support price policies have allocated resources away from these high demand growth sectors. This has made inflation in food prices more intense.

In addition to the above, agricultural growth has lagged significantly behind the growth in the non-agricultural part of the economy. Between 2000-2001 and 2012-2013, non-agricultural GDP grew at an average annual rate of almost 8 per cent while agriculture grew at about 3 per cent, a considerable disparity. However, the growth of agriculture during this period was high in comparison to previous years. Even more important, the increase in yields has slowed dramatically. Data concerning these trends are presented in table 6.

As indicated in the table, rice and wheat production growth rates declined significantly, despite the application of minimum support prices, but rice yields grew only slightly and wheat yields declined. The production of fruit and vegetables was in accordance with the growth of demand, but yield growth of vegetables remained sluggish or actually fell.

Table 6. Annual growth of production and yields

Crop	Production		Yields	
	1990s	2000s	1990s	2000s
Rice	1.79	0.87	1.40	1.50
Wheat	4.36	0.57	2.90	1.10
Pulses	-0.39	1.88	1.80	1.20
Fruits	4.20	5.80	0.70	0.70
Vegetables	4.20	5.40	3.20	1.70

Source: Adapted from Bhattacharya, Rao and Gupta (2014).

Thus, technical innovation has slowed dramatically in agriculture relative to the pace experienced during the "Green Revolution". Public expenditures in agriculture as a share of GDP remained stagnant in the 1990s and 2000s at about 2 to 3 per cent per year. Even more importantly, these public expenditures have been increasingly devoted to subsidies rather than the development of new technologies. By 2009-2010, nearly 80 per cent of public sector spending was in the form of subsidies. While power subsidies remained around 5 per cent of agricultural GDP from the mid-1990s to the late 2000s, fertilizer subsidies increased dramatically, jumping from about 1.7 per cent of agricultural GDP to about 8 per cent. The result is that technical innovation in agriculture has slowed considerably. Thus, the growth in demand for food items was met by sluggish growth in agricultural productivity. This, in turn, led to rapidly rising food prices with a corresponding effect on real wages in agriculture and non-agriculture sectors (Bhattacharya, Rao and Gupta, 2014).

Based on the above-mentioned analysis, it can be argued that real wages have been driven up as a result of a rise, over time, of food prices. However, there is another factor that has influenced real wages more directly, namely the Mahatma Gandhi National Rural Employment Guarantee Scheme (MGNREGS). The main objective of this programme was to enhance the economic stability of rural household income by providing at least 100 days of guaranteed employment to every household. This mainly involved unskilled manual labour. The programme was initially introduced in parts of India in 2006 and extended to all of the country by 2008 (Bhattacharya, Rao and Gupta, 2014).

This type of programme directly adds to upward pressure on the wage through an increase in the demand for labour. This, in turn, tends to boost the bargaining power of rural, unskilled workers, putting upward pressure on the real wage earned in agriculture, as well as on wages in manufacturing, especially those associated with labour-intensive manufacturing. These types of economic activities intensively require the use of lesser skilled labour, which is abundant in the countryside of India (Guha and Tripathi, 2014).

A number of papers have indeed found that this programme has exerted upward pressure on real wages. For example, Imbert and Papp (2012) used data from National Sample Survey Office (NSSO) to conclude that MGNREGS raised public works employment by 0.3 person day per month and casual wage income by 4.5 per cent. Berg and others (2012) used data from Agricultural Wages in India to find that MGNREGS increased agricultural wage rates by 5.3 per cent. As Gulati, Jain and Satiga (2013) noted, a 10 per cent increase in employment had pushed up agricultural wages by 0.3 per cent to 0.8 per cent. Thus, the empirical evidence indicates that the increased demand from this programme pushed up wages in rural areas in India.

It is not being argued in this paper that the employment guarantee scheme of India has reduced the welfare of unskilled workers in India. It seems that the opposite has occurred; their real earnings rose. The point being made here is that a side effect of this policy has been to make it more difficult for labour-intensive manufacturing to succeed. This would not have occurred if the productivity of agriculture had expanded in tandem with the employment guarantee. If this were to occur, labour costs associated with labour-intensive manufacturing would not need to increase and, consequently, the latter would not face increased difficulty in terms of being profitable. In addition, the increased income of unskilled workers would likely increase the demand for labour-intensive manufactured goods.

In this section, it has been argued that the process of structural change in India is much different from the process in many other countries or subregions, such as East Asia, China, and parts of South-East Asia. Typically, as economic growth occurs, the proportion of GDP and employment connected with agriculture declines (with the former generally falling more rapidly than the latter, at least initially). This is generally accompanied by rapid growth in labour-intensive manufacturing followed quickly by rapid growth in the modern service sector, with the share of these sectors in employment and GDP increasing. In India, labour-intensive manufacturing has not followed this pattern.

The simple reason offered for this phenomenon has been that the rise in the wage to capital rent ratio has resulted in labour becoming relatively more expensive relative to capital. This has occurred as a result of the decline in the rental rate of capital and a rise in the real wage rate of labour. This paper focuses on analysing the latter factor, the rise of real wages. Specifically, it was argued that rise in food prices driven by demand stemming from economic growth has resulted in rising real wages.

The sluggishness in supply response to this growing demand is the critical factor. Supply side sluggishness is the result of slow rates of technical innovation in agriculture combined with the distortions created by the minimum support price policies adopted by the state. This has been exacerbated by an employment guarantee scheme. Again, to emphasize, the underlying problem is that the supply side of food production has not kept up with the growing demand.

In order to further test the ideas developed above, some additional empirical analysis was carried out. Lacking adequate data on wages for a long period, it was not possible to examine the impact of food prices on wages. However, adequate data are available for an examination of the relationship between food price increases and the share of manufacturing in GDP relative to the share of services in GDP. The equation that was estimated can be written as

$$\text{MfgS/ServS} = \beta_0 + \beta_1\,(\text{MfgS/ServS})_{t-1} + \beta_2\,\text{CPIIWF} + \beta_3\,\text{GDPPGR} + \varepsilon \qquad (2)$$

where MfgS/ServS is the share of manufacturing in GDP divided by the share of services in GDP, $(\text{MfgS/ServS})_{t-1}$ is the same variable lagged one time period, CPIIWF is the consumer price index for food for industrial workers, and GDPPGR is the growth rate of real per capita GDP. The data for GDP shares and growth of GDP per capita were taken from World Development Indicators. The data for CPIIWF come from the work of Sasmal (2015). The time period covered is from 1971 to 2012. It is expected that more rapid growth in real GDP per capita would be positively related to the ratio of the share of manufacturing in GDP to that of services, namely manufacturing would become more important (at least initially). The lagged value of the independent variable is included on the right hand side in order to reduce serial correlation. Finally, the argument made in this paper would imply that higher food prices would be associated with a reduction in the share of manufacturing relative to services in GDP.

The results of the estimation are presented in table 7. As indicated, the sign on GDPPGR is positive, but it is not statistically significant. The sign on CPIIWF is negative and statistically significant, as hypothesized. Thus, rising food prices are associated with a decline in the importance of manufacturing relative to services.

**Table 7. Estimation results: manufacturing as a share
of GDP relative to services as a share of GDP
as the dependent variable**

Variable	Coefficient
$(MfgS/ServS)_{t-1}$	0.6662***
	(0.113)
CPIIWF	-0.00008***
	(0.00003)
GDPPGR	0.02697
	(0.07877)
Constant	0.1333**
	(0.04528)
Observations	40

Notes: Standard error for each coefficient value is given in parentheses.

** Signifies significance at the 5% level, and *** signifies significance
at the 1% level.

IV. SUMMARY AND CONCLUSION

Structural change in India and the particular path it has taken has been the focus of this paper. Theoretical models, including a food production sector, manufacturing and services (both modern and traditional) were constructed. The implication of those models was that a rise in food prices will, among other things, cause resources to flow out of manufacturing. In particular, wages would rise in agriculture, drawing labour out of manufacturing and into food-producing agriculture. However, the increased wage rate is likely to lead to increased mechanization of agriculture in the long run, implying that the growth in employment opportunities in this sector may slow. Thus, labour-intensive informal service activities in rural areas are likely to grow. This occurs even in an open economy context in which the large country case is assumed. A second model incorporating modern services as the export sector (human capital intensive) has a similar implication. Expansion in this sector (growth in income) would lead to an increase in expenditures on manufacturing and food. The manufactured goods would be increasingly imported as the real wage in agriculture is driven up and labour flows into food production and rural-based informal service production and away from manufacturing. The overall conclusion is that as long as food productivity remains sluggish, economic growth would increase the relative cost of labour and labour-intensive manufacturing would be less and less likely to be competitive. Thus, growth would not generate rapid expansion in employment.

The experience of India was utilized to illustrate the process outlined in the theory. Evidence was presented to show that labour had become relatively more expensive, reducing labour-intensive manufacturing. The rise in the relative price of labour was shown to be partly the result of rising food prices stemming from rapid growth in demand (stimulated by overall growth) compared to sluggish growth in agricultural productivity. These trends were exacerbated by the minimum price support policy and the employment guarantee programme. The latter may have enhanced the welfare of unskilled rural labour, but the unexpected consequence was rising food prices and rural labour becoming more expensive. These effects would have been mitigated by rapid growth in agricultural productivity.

Before closing, it should be pointed out that the ability of increased agricultural productivity, especially in food, to enhance the development of manufacturing through relatively cheap food may be limited by the existing structure of the economy. Countries that have already developed substantial modern service sectors, such as India, and have bypassed labour-intensive manufacturing may find it difficult to shift to an alternative path. Broad-based development may, as a result, involve creating a high wage, highly productive agricultural sector with a rural-based highly productive service sector. Agriculture would continue to employ a high share of the population for some time with income per person in that sector approaching the rate earned in urban areas. This kind of development path is being examined in some of the most recent research (Dorin, Hourcade and Benoit-Cattin, 2013).

REFERENCE

Amirapu, Amrit, and Arvind Subramanian (2015). Manufacturing or services? An Indian illustration of a development dilemma. Working Paper, No. 409. Washington, D.C.: Center for Global Development.

Baldwin, Richard (2011). Trade and industrialisation after globalisation's 2nd unbundling: how building and joining a supply chain are different and why it matters. Working Paper, No. 17716. Cambridge, MA: National Bureau of Economic Research.

Berg, Erlend, and others (2012). Can rural public works affect agricultural wages? Evidence from India. Working Paper Series, WPS/2012-05. Oxford, U.K.: Centre for the Study of African Economies, Oxford University.

Bhattacharya Rudrani, Narhari Rao, and Abhijit Sen Gupta (2014). Understanding food inflation in India. South Asia Working Paper Series, No. 26. Manila: Asian Development Bank.

Binswanger-Mkhize, Hans Peter, and Alwin D'Sousa (2011). Structural transformation of the Indian economy and its agriculture. In *Productivity Growth in Agriculture: An International Perspective*, K.O. Fuglie, S.L. Wang and V. Eldin Ball, eds. Oxfordshire, U.K.: CAB International.

Dorin, Bruno, Jean-Charles Hourcade, and Michel Benoit-Cattin (2013). A world without farmers? The Lewis path revisited. Working Paper, No. 24-2013. Nogent-sur-Marne, France: Centre International de Recherches sur l'Environnement et le Developpement.

Felipe, Jesus, Aashish Mehta, and Changyong Rhee (2014). Manufacturing matters...but it's the jobs that count. Economics Working Paper Series, No. 420. Manila: Asian Development Bank.

Gollin, Douglas, Remi Jedwab, and Dietrich Vollrath (2013). Urbanization with and without industrialization. *Journal of Economic Growth*, vol. 21, No. 21, pp. 35-70.

Gollin, Douglas, Stephen L. Parentz, and Richard. Rogerson (2007). The food problem and the evolution of international income levels. *Journal of Monetary Economics*, vol. 54, Issue 4, pp. 1230-1255.

Guha, Atulan, and Ashutosk K.R. Tripathi (2014). Link between food price inflation and rural wage dynamic. *Economic and Political Weekly*, vol. 49, No. 26 and 27, pp. 66-72.

Gulati, Ashok, Surbhi Jain, and Nidhi Satiga (2013). Rising farm wages in India: the 'pull' and 'push' factors. Discussion Paper, No. 5. New Delhi: Commission for Agricultural Costs and Prices.

Imbert, Clément, and John Papp (2012). Equilibrium distributional impacts of government employment programs: evidence from India's employment guarantee. Paris School of Economic Working Paper, No. 2012-2014. Paris: Centre National de la Recherche Scientifique.

Jacoby, Hanan (2013). Food prices, wages, and welfare in rural India. Policy Research Working Paper, No. 6412. Washington, D.C.: World Bank.

Kochhar, Kalpana, and others (2006). India's pattern of development: what happened, what follows? *Journal of Monetary Economics*, vol. 53, No. 5, pp. 981-1019.

Lewis, W. Arthur (1954). Economic development with unlimited supplies of labour. *The Manchester School*, vol. 22, No. 2, pp. 139-191.

Reddy, Amarender (2015). Growth, structural change, wage rates in rural India. *Economic and Political Weekly*, vol. 1, No. 2, pp. 56-65 (January), pp. 56-65.

Ricardo, David (1965). *On the Principles of Political Economy and Taxation*. London: Everyman's Library.

Rodrik, Dani (2013). Unconditional convergence in manufacturing. *Quarterly Journal of Economics*, vol. 128, No. 1, pp. 165-204.

_____ (2014). Has sustained growth decoupled from industrialization? Presentation presented at the Frontier Issues in Economic Growth: A Symposium from the Growth Dialogue. George Washington University, Washington, D.C., 10 February. Available from https://dinmerican.wordpress.com/2014/04/09/dani-rodrik-has-sustained-growth-decoupled-from-industrialization/.

Sasmal, Joydeb (2015). Food price inflation in India: the growing economy with sluggish agriculture. *Journal of Economics, Finance and Administrative Science*, vol. 20, No. 38, pp. 30-40.

Sen, Kunal, and Deb Kusum Das (2014). Where have all the workers gone? The puzzle of declining labor intensity in organized Indian manufacturing. Development Economics and Public Policy Working Paper Series, No. 35/2014. Manchester: University of Manchester, Institute for Development Policy and Management.

Van Campenhout, Bjorn, Karl Pauw, and Nicholas Minot (2013). The impact of food price shocks in Uganda: first order versus long-run effects. Discussion Paper, 01284. Washington, D.C.: International Food Policy Research Institute.

Wiggins, Steve, and Sharada Keats (2014). *Rural Wages in Asia*. London: Overseas Development Institute.

THE IMPACTS OF CLIMATIC AND NON-CLIMATIC FACTORS ON HOUSEHOLD FOOD SECURITY: A STUDY ON THE POOR LIVING IN THE MALAYSIAN EAST COAST ECONOMIC REGION

*Md. Mahmudul Alam, Chamhuri Siwar and Abu N.M. Wahid**

Sustainable food security at the household level is a national concern in many countries. The reasons for household food insecurity include, among others, social, economic, political, and personal factors, as well as climatic changes and its outcomes. This research aims to determine the linkage of the factors of climatic changes, non-climatic factors and household resiliencies with the level of household food security among the poor and low income households in Malaysia. The present study is based on primary data that were collected in July and October 2012 through a questionnaire survey of 460 poor and low-income households from the Pahang, Kelantan, and Terengganu States of Malaysia. The sample was selected from E-Kasih poor household database based on a cluster random sampling technique. Initially the study measures household food security according to the United States Agency for International Development – Household Food Insecurity Access (USAID-HFIA) model, and has run ordinal regressions under the logit and probit models. This study finds that household food insecurity is not only linked with social and economic factors, but also significantly linked with the climatic factors. Therefore, food security programmes must be integrated with the programmes for climatic change adaptation.

*   Md. Mahmudul Alam, corresponding author, Senior Lecturer, School of Economics, Finance and Banking (SEFB), College of Business (COB), Universiti Utara Malaysia (UUM), Sintok, Kedah, Malaysia (e-mail: rony000@gmail.com); Chamhuri Siwar, Emeritus Professor, Institute for Environment and Development (LESTARI), National University of Malaysia (UKM), 43600 UKM Bangi, Selangor Darul Ehsan, Malaysia (e-mail: csiwar@ukm.my); and Abu N.M. Wahid, Professor, Department of Economics and Finance, Tennessee State University, Nashville, Tennessee, United States (e-mail: awahid@tnstate.edu). We are thankful to the Ministry of Science, Technology and Environment of Malaysia for generously funding the research under the Fundamental Research Grant Scheme of the Malaysian Ministry of Higher Education (FRGS/1/2012/SS07/UKM/01/3) and UKM Arus Perdana Research Grant Project (AP-2014-017).

JEL classification: I32, Q54, P48.

Keywords: Climatic changes, household food security, poverty, ordinal regression, resilience, East Coast Economic Region, Malaysia.

I. INTRODUCTION

The 2008 global food crisis serves as a prelude to a more acute food crisis in the future. As a result, food security is a national issue for many countries. The major food security concern is about making agricultural production sufficient for domestic consumption and having the capability to access food in the international markets.

Sustainable food security at the household level is also equally important because national food security is not enough to ensure sustainable food security at the household level. The drivers of household food security are in fact more crucial at the national level as food security is defined in its most basic form as access by all people at all times to food needed for a healthy life (FAO, 2003, p. 28). As such, the focus of food security should be on the household as the basic unit in the society. This distinction is important because activities directed towards improving household food security may be quite different from those aimed at improving food security in general.

There are many factors that drive household food insecurity. According to Lovendal and Knowles (2006), these factors include political, economic, environment, natural, social, infrastructural and health issues. Frankenberger (1992) puts forward that assets, community inequalities, risk-minimizing strategies and coping strategy are also important drivers. Nyariki and Wiggins (1997) give utilization of physical, natural, and human resources, availability of technology, and off-farm jobs as factors that drive household to food insecurity. Negatu (2006) mentions that major drivers are capability to produce one's own food and growth of purchasing power. Iram and Butt (2004), ECA (2004), Cristofar and Basiotis (1992), and Olson and others (1997) and Rose and Basiotis (1995) add household's demography, access to land, land tenure system, ability to utilize the land productively, and savings to the list of factors. Other researchers, such as Fartahun and others (2007), Hindin (2006), Myntti (1993), Pfeiffer, Gloyd and Li (2001), Piaseu (2006) and Negatu (2006), widen the list to include women with income-earning capability, women's education, sufficient income, number of children, social support, accessibility to productive resources, educational level, landholdings, accessibility to transport, livestock productivity, awareness of suitable interventions, storage technology, and unemployment level.

Changes in the climatic factors and its outcomes would also affect household food security. According to the Intergovernmental Panel on Climate Change (IPCC) and Fourth Assessment Report, food security and malnutrition are likely to be severely affected by climate change and variability (IPCC, 2007). FAO (2007; 2008) has also stressed that climate change affects the availability of food, food supply stability, accessibility to food and utilization of food. This, in turn, results in negative effects on nutrition and food security. Water scarcity and droughts reduce the nutritional diversity and decrease general food consumption, which leads to malnutrition, such as micronutrient deficiencies, protein-energy malnutrition and under nutrition (IPCC, 2007). An increase in rainfall, temperature, sea levels and salinity give rise to flooding in human settlement areas (Cruz and others, 2007; Mimura and others, 2007). It may also cause scarcity of freshwater (Kundzewicz and others, 2007) and increased occurrences of diarrhea and other contagious diseases (Checkley and others, 2000; Kovats and others, 2004; Zimmerman and others, 2007). Climatic changes also affect food distribution, as it may hinder access to markets to sell or purchase food (Abdulai and CroleRees, 2001), put upward pressure on food prices (Cline, 2007; von Braun 2007) and reduce real income (Thomson and Metz, 1998).

Malaysia is a rapidly developing country with a fairly diversified economy. According to EIA (2005), carbon dioxide (CO_2) emissions in Malaysia have increased by 221 per cent during the 1990-2004 period. The country is now one of the 30 largest greenhouse gas emitters. Global warming is expected to elevate the temperature by $0.3\text{-}4.5^\circ C$. Warmer temperature will cause sea level to rise by about 95 cm over a hundred-year period and changes in rainfall between -30 per cent to +30 per cent. It will lead to a reduction in crop yield and cause drought in many areas, making it difficult to cultivate some crops (MOSTE, 2001). Moreover, projections indicate that maximum monthly precipitation will increase by 51 per cent in Pahang, Kelantan and Terengganu, while minimum precipitation will decrease between 32 per cent and 61 per cent for the whole Peninsular Malaysia. Consequently, annual rainfall may increase by up to 10 per cent in Kelantan, Terengganu, Pahang and North-West Coast, and decrease by up to 5 per cent in Selangor and Johor (NAHRIM, 2006). Tisdell (1996) finds that rainfall variability increases the level of environmental stress that affects the capability of the system to maintain productivity.

Under the current climate change scenario, temperatures above $25^\circ C$ may reduce grain mass by 4.4 per cent per $1^\circ C$ rise (Tashiro and Wardlaw, 1989), and grain yield may decline as much as by 9.6-10.0 per cent per $1^\circ C$ rise (Baker and Allen, 1993). Singh and others (1996) reveal that the actual farm yields of rice in Malaysia vary from 3 to 5 tons per hectare, where potential yield is 7.2 tons. The study also unfolds that there is a decline in rice yield between 4.6 per cent and 6.1 per cent per $1^\circ C$ temperature increase and a doubling of CO_2 concentration (from present level of 340 ppm to 680 ppm), which may offset the detrimental effect of a $4^\circ C$ temperature increase on rice production in Malaysia. Overall, based on the analysis of minimum and maximum yield over the last 28 years, the macro cases of the Malaysian national data from 1980 to 2008 show that the yield of paddy would decrease between 43 per cent and 61 per cent if there is a 1°C temperature and 1 millimeter (mm) rainfall increase (Ali and Ali, 2009). A recent study, based on the micro data on paddy field of the Integrated Agricultural Development Area (IADA), has indicated that in North-West Selangor, a temperature increase of 1 per cent may lead to a 3.44 per cent decrease in current paddy yield and a 0.03 per cent decrease in paddy yield in the following season, and that if rainfall were to increase by 1 per cent, paddy yield might decrease by 0.12 per cent and then another 0.12 per cent in the following season (Alam and others, 2014).

Malaysia joined 185 other nations in signing the Declaration of Rome at the 1996 International Food Summit, pledging to reduce the prevalence of hunger by at least 50 per cent, within its own jurisdiction by a target date sometime in the early 21st century. However, in Malaysia, food security has been embedded into the theme of the self-sufficiency level that referred to paddy or rice sector only (Arshad, Shamsudin and Saleh, 1999; Alam and others, 2011; 2012b), instead of having a specific or special policy on overall food security. To ensure food security in Malaysia, the Government has adopted two strategies, establishing a self-sufficiency level and building rice stocks both domestically and internationally. However, the country has yet to meet the food self-sufficiency level. About 10 to 35 per cent of the total rice requirement is imported from neighbouring countries, namely India, Myanmar, Pakistan and Viet Nam. Thus far, the highest food self-sufficiency level for the country was 95 per cent, recorded in 1975, and the lowest was 65 per cent, recorded in 1990.

As climate change is one of the major potential threats to the national food security in Malaysia, there is a strong possibility that climatic change is linked to the household food security of the country. To ensure food security and proper policy options in Malaysia, it is very important to study the current situation of household food security and the linkage between the changes in climatic factors and sustainable food security at the household level. Very few studies have been conducted on the impacts of changes in climatic factors and its outcomes on household food security in Malaysia (Alam and others, 2016a; 2016b). Hence, the present paper is an attempt to conduct an in-depth study on this issue. The findings of this study may be helpful for policymakers in their efforts towards setting targets in national development plans on food security, socioeconomic betterment, poverty alleviation, and achieve *Vision 2020* – to become a fully developed country by 2020.

II. DATA, MODEL AND METHODOLOGY

Data collection

For the empirical assessment, this study mostly relies on primary data collected through an extensive questionnaire survey at the household level in the East Coast Economic Region (ECER) in Malaysia. ECER was selected as the study area because it covers more than half of the Peninsular Malaysia, comprising an area of about 66,000 square kilometres that includes the states of Kelantan, Terengganu and Pahang, and the district of Mersing in Johor (figure 1). ECER is very crucial for two major reasons: (a) ECER is the most vulnerable area in Malaysia to climatic changes; and (b) the income level of this area is low and the poverty rate is high, providing a hindrance to the drive to achieve *Vision 2020* (Alam and others, 2012a; ECERDC, 2007; 2008). The population of ECER was about 3.95 million in 2005, which represented 14.8 per cent of the total population of Malaysia. In 2004 the incidences of poverty were 10.6 per cent, 4 per cent, and 15.4 per cent in Kelantan, Pahang, and Terengganu, respectively, whereas for the country as a whole, it was 5.7 per cent, while the incidences of hard-core poverty were 1.3 per cent, 1.0 per cent, and 4.4 per cent for the three states, respectively, as compared to 1.2 per cent for the country as a whole. At that time, there were about 45,000 paddy farmers in ECER, and the average productivity per worker was 11,915 Malaysian ringgit (RM) ($3,135),[1] while the national agriculture productivity per worker was RM15,355 ($4,040).[1]

The East Coast Economic Region is mainly agricultural. In 2004, crops production covered a total area of 2.22 million ha in ECER (34.8 per cent of the Peninsular Malaysia). However, in 2008, the Government officially launched a very large project to develop five key areas – manufacturing, oil, gas and petrochemicals, tourism, agriculture and human capital development. With the objective to fast-forward the inflow of foreign direct investment (FDI) and industrialization in the region; the ECER Special Economic Zone (ECER SEZ) and Malaysia-China Kuantan Industrial Park were initiated in this area. Consequently, projects worth an estimated RM112 billion in value are expected to be implemented in ECER by 2020. The ECER Special Economic Zone is expected to generate up to RM90 billion in investments and contribute RM23 billion ($5.2 billion) to the national GDP, as well as create 220,000 jobs, out of the 560,000 jobs identified.

---

[1] The dollar amount is based on the historical Malaysian ringgit per US dollar rate of 3.8 for 2004.

Figure 1. Location of the study area (ECER-Malaysia)

Source: Alam and others (2012a).

Note: The boundaries and names shown and the designations used on this map do not imply official
         endorsement or acceptance by the United Nations.

The study follows a two-stage cluster random sampling technique. Initially, the samples are clustered by location and then by poverty category. Finally, from each category, samples are picked randomly from the *E-Kasih* database, which is an integrated database system that enlists poor households at the national level to plan, implement and monitor poverty programmes. The urban area of Kuantan and rural area of Pekan were selected in Pahang State. The urban area of Kota Bharu and rural area of Tumpat were chosen from Kelantan State. The urban area of Kuala Terengganu and rural area of Marang were included from Terengganu State.

Based on the formula of required size of samples (Yamane, 1967, p. 886), first, 400 households are selected according to the proportion of population distribution. However, to ensure a good number of observations for each group, which is needed to conduct a sound statistical analysis for any particular group, another 100 households have been added to the sample. However, while targeting the sample size to be 500, after collecting and validating the data, 460 households remain in the sample. The final distribution of the collected sample is given in table 1.

Table 1. Distribution of the sample of the study

	Pahang		Kelantan		Terengganu		Total		All
	Urban	Rural	Urban	Rural	Urban	Rural	Urban	Rural	Total
Hard-core poor	2	15	33	22	6	32	41	69	110
Poor	12	14	21	34	27	46	60	94	154
Recently marginally non-poor	11	9	15	16	4	16	30	41	71
Marginally non-poor	18	30	32	25	4	16	54	71	125
Total target group	43	68	101	97	41	110	185	275	460
State total	111		198		151		460		

Note: * In the *E-Kasih* system, the rural poverty data were categorized as monthly income per person: up to
         RM110 was hard-core poor, up to RM185 was poor, and up to RM227 was marginally non-poor, and for
         urban area up to RM120 was hard-core poor, up to RM200 was poor, and up to RM340 was marginally
         non-poor.

A face-to-face interview based on a structured questionnaire is used to collect data. The survey was conducted by the regular enumerators of the Implementation Coordination Unit (ICU) agency from Pahang, Kelantan, and Terengganu during July and October in 2012.

Model specification

To measure the relationship between household status of food security and the climatic and general factors affecting on food security, the following *ordered dependent regression* or *ordinal regression* is conducted based on *logit* and *probit* models:

$$Z_i = (Y1, Y2)$$

$$X_i = (X1, ..., X63)$$

$$Z_i = f(X_i) \tag{1}$$

In the study, the two dependent variables, the household status of food accessibility and household food availability, are used as the measurements of household food security. Household food availability is based on measurement on the direct perception of the household, while household status of food accessibility measurement is based on the frequency of calculation. To measure the status of household food availability, households are asked about their food status in the previous month (see table 2). To measure the status of household food accessibility, this study applies direct measuring questionnaire-based techniques developed by Coates, Swindale and Bilinsky (2007) for United States Agency for International

Development (USAID), which is known as Household Food Insecurity Access (HFIA) (table 3).

The list of the independent variables of the study (see appendix) consists of different resilience factors of a household (X1-X18), non-climatic factors (X18-X44) and climatic factors (X45-X63). These variables are considered from the four dimensions of food security – availability of food, stability of supply, accessibility to food, and utilization of food (FAO, 2005; 2008). The availability of food means sufficient quantities of quality food available at the household level. The accessibility of food means household's access to sufficient resources, including a set of the commodity bundles that an individual can access based on the legal, economic, political, and social arrangement of a community in which they live for getting quality foods for a nutritious meal. Food utilization shows the significance of non-food inputs in food security, such as proper diet, clean water, health care and sanitation, to gain nutritional well-being in which all physiological requirements are met. Food system stability refers to households having access to sufficient food at all times even to the point that they would have access to food during a sudden crisis, such as one that is economic or climate-related, or a cyclical occurrence, such as seasonal food insecurities. Here, the resilience refers to the households' capacity or strength to cope with stress and hardship in case of actual or expected food insecurity, which are categorized as socioeconomic, physical assets, and livelihood strategy and behaviour. The measurements of all variables are given in the appendix.

To check the best fit model and robustness, the study reports both the probit and logit models, but for analysis, it mostly focuses on the logit model. Logit and probit models that look like a sigmoid function with a domain between 0 and 1, which makes them both quantile functions based on the assumption that the logit model follows logistic distribution and the probit model follows a normal distribution. Normally, the logit model is used when every observation has equal probability. Furthermore, a correlation analysis is undertaken to determine the relationship among the relevant variables and to check the multicollinearity problem. Finally, this study also justifies how the endogeneity and causality problems are considered.

III. RESULTS AND DISCUSSION

Measurement of household food security

In terms of household food availability, 14.8 per cent stated that they had enough food that they liked, but a large number of the households (41.1 per cent) indicated that they did not always have enough food that they liked, while 9.1 per cent of the households stated that they frequently remained hungry (table 2).

Table 2. Family food status in the previous month

Food status in the family	No. of households	% of total
Enough of the kinds of food you want to eat	68	14.8
Enough but not always the kinds of food you want to eat	189	41.1
Sometimes not enough to eat	100	21.7
Often not enough to eat	61	13.3
Frequently hungry	42	9.1
Total	**460**	**100.0**

Household food insecurity access (calculated for each household by assigning a code 1-4, where 1 = food secure access, 2 = mildly food insecure access, 3 = moderately food insecure access, 4 = severely food insecure access. Initially, the data are coded frequency-of-occurrence as 0 for all cases where the answer to the corresponding occurrence question is "no", namely if Q1 = 0, then Q1a = 0, etc.). Then, the intensities of the occurrence of nine questions are measured in three frequencies – rarely (1-2 times per month) or sometimes (3-10 times) or often (10+ times per month) – which is indicated by Q1a to Q9a (table 3). Finally, the four food accessibility categories are created sequentially to ensure that households are classified according to their most severe response.

- Category = 1 if [(Q1 = 0 or Q1 = 1) and Q2 = 0 and Q3 = 0 and Q4 = 0 and Q5 = 0 and Q6 = 0 and Q7 = 0 and Q8 = 0 and Q9 = 0]

- Category = 2 if [(Q1a = 2 or Q1a = 3 or Q2a = 1 or Q2a = 2 or Q2a = 3 or Q3a = 1 or Q4a = 1) and Q5 = 0 and Q6 = 0 and Q7= 0 and Q8 = 0 and Q9 = 0]

- Category = 3 if [(Q3a = 2 or Q3a = 3 or Q4a = 2 or Q4a = 3 or Q5a = 1 or Q5a = 2 or Q6a = 1 or Q6a = 2) and Q7 = 0 and Q8 = 0 and Q9 = 0]

- Category = 4 if [Q5a = 3 or Q6a = 3 or Q7a = 1 or Q7a = 2 or Q7a = 3 or Q8a = 1 or Q8a = 2 or Q8a = 3 or Q9a = 1 or Q9a = 2 or Q9a = 3]

The following table illustrates the above four categorizations in which every household is placed in a unique category based on the set of the responses (table 3).

Based on the survey, this study finds that 52.8 per cent of the households are under the category of "food secure access". Among the surveyed households,

23.3 per cent are facing mildly food insecurity (access), who are worried about not having enough food sometimes or often, and/or are unable to eat preferred foods, and/or rarely eat a more monotonous diet than desired and/or also rarely eat some undesirable foods (table 4).

Table 3. Measurement of the Household Food Insecurity Access Scale (HFIAS)

HFIAS measurement issues	Category of food insecurity (access)		
	Rarely (1-2 times per month)	Sometimes (3-10 times)	Often (10+ times per month)
Q1 Worry about food			
Q2 Unable to eat prefer food			
Q3 Eat just a few kinds of foods			
Q4 Eat foods they really do not want eat			
Q5 Eat a smaller meal			
Q6 Eat fewer meals in a day			
Q7 No food of any kinds in the household			
Q8 Go to sleep hungry			
Q9 Go through the whole day and night without eating			
Food secure access	Mildly food insecure	Moderately food insecure	Severely food insecure

Sources: Coates, Swindale and Bilinsky (2007); Alam and others (2016b).

Table 4. Distribution of Household Food Insecurity Access (HFIA)

HFIA category	HFIA prevalence	% of HFIA prevalence
1 = Food secure access	243	52.8
2 = Mildly food insecure access	107	23.3
3 = Moderately food insecure access	66	14.3
4 = Severely food insecure access	44	9.6
Total	**460**	**100.0**

Among the households, 14.3 per cent are moderately food insecure. These households frequently sacrifice quality of food by eating a monotonous diet or undesirable foods sometimes or often, and/or reduce eating the quantity of food rarely or sometimes. Some 9.6 per cent of households are severely food insecure and consequently, need to cut back on meal size or the number of meals, and/or experience any of the three most severe conditions – running out of food, going to bed hungry or going a whole day and night without eating.

Household status of food security and relevant factors

The regression models based on equation 1 show that some of the resilience factors have a statistically significant relationship with household food availability and food accessibility (table 5). The P-values of the likelihood ratio (LR) statistics for both models, which are shown below at 0.0000001, suggest a very good fit of the models. The pseudo R-squares are 0.354 for food availability and 0.305 for the food accessibility models.

Results for household food availability (Y1) models indicate that the climatic impacts on kitchen environment (X58) and sanitation system (X60) are statistically significant. Among the non-climatic/general factors, competition for common resources (X31), common resources dependency for cattle or livestock feeding (X30), incidences of diseases, such as dengue, malaria, heat stretch, cold and skin disease (X44), having knowledge about taking precaution against dengue, malaria (X17), buying bulk amount of food (X12), household poverty/economic status (X3), earning ratio (X6), and number of school going children (X2) are statistically significant.

Table 5. Relationship between household status of food security and relevant climatic and non-climatic/general factors

Variable	Dependent variable Y1				Dependent variable Y2			
	Ordered probit		Ordered logit		Ordered probit		Ordered logit	
	Odds ratio	Prob.	Odds ratio	Prob.	Odds ratio	Prob.	Odds ratio	Prob.
Household resilience factors: socioeconomic								
X1	1.114	0.449	1.302	0.318	0.994	0.956	1.004	0.981
X2	0.722*	0.007	0.528*	0.005	0.652*	0.000	0.486*	0.000
X3	0.739*	0.002	0.590*	0.003	0.821*	0.004	0.719*	0.005
X4	1.264	0.467	1.822	0.306	2.315*	0.002	4.191*	0.002
X5	0.982	0.964	0.846	0.828	0.865	0.558	0.760	0.521
X6	1.181	0.136	1.412***	0.092	1.385*	0.001	1.800*	0.001
X7	1.193	0.542	1.404	0.521	1.489***	0.093	1.811	0.146
Household resilience factors: physical assets								
X8	0.830	0.467	0.690	0.430	1.275	0.195	1.473	0.222
X9	1.065	0.825	1.017	0.974	1.289	0.210	1.466	0.278
X10	0.857	0.294	0.741	0.263	1.044	0.684	1.104	0.592
X11	1.445	0.176	1.801	0.232	1.797*	0.002	2.769*	0.001

Table 5. *(continued)*

Variable	Dependent variable Y1				Dependent variable Y2			
	Ordered probit		Ordered logit		Ordered probit		Ordered logit	
	Odds ratio	Prob.	Odds ratio	Prob.	Odds ratio	Prob.	Odds ratio	Prob.
Household resilience factors: livelihood strategy and behaviour								
X12	2.098*	0.006	4.046*	0.006	1.057	0.754	1.080	0.796
X13	1.074	0.623	1.144	0.631	1.051	0.634	1.091	0.624
X14	1.220	0.221	1.444	0.220	1.194	0.153	1.333	0.182
X15	0.782	0.269	0.632	0.274	1.119	0.456	1.202	0.478
X16	1.085	0.616	1.139	0.665	1.049	0.683	1.074	0.724
X17	1.673**	0.039	2.602**	0.035	1.026	0.851	1.058	0.809
Non-climatic factors								
X18	0.839	0.318	0.657	0.182	1.035	0.775	1.028	0.892
X19	1.212	0.201	1.475	0.165	1.022	0.851	1.041	0.836
X20	1.222	0.228	1.500	0.194	0.992	0.944	0.994	0.977
X21	1.079	0.677	1.144	0.688	1.051	0.675	1.109	0.603
X22	0.828	0.299	0.676	0.234	0.791***	0.079	0.663***	0.073
X23	1.114	0.495	1.246	0.444	0.760**	0.018	0.630**	0.019
X24	1.087	0.485	1.169	0.473	0.947	0.543	0.936	0.660
X25	1.168	0.301	1.417	0.219	1.038	0.740	1.077	0.697
X26	0.873	0.290	0.772	0.268	0.809**	0.022	0.682**	0.016
X27	1.075	0.657	1.155	0.624	1.100	0.385	1.183	0.365
X28	0.933	0.649	0.876	0.645	0.945	0.617	0.913	0.631
X29	1.235	0.123	1.355	0.221	0.917	0.401	0.846	0.349
X30	1.343**	0.041	1.823**	0.025	0.967	0.751	0.927	0.674
X31	0.803***	0.092	0.662***	0.076	1.127	0.227	1.246	0.199
X32	1.084	0.526	1.133	0.600	1.023	0.830	1.046	0.807
X33	0.855	0.302	0.710	0.226	1.062	0.598	1.140	0.504
X34	0.820	0.252	0.693	0.245	0.840	0.211	0.763	0.259
X35	1.121	0.527	1.288	0.451	0.877	0.369	0.755	0.268
X36	0.935	0.680	0.877	0.661	0.833	0.130	0.731	0.127
X37	0.959	0.786	0.919	0.764	1.175	0.177	1.328	0.164
X38	1.148	0.418	1.200	0.565	1.180	0.190	1.319	0.197
X39	1.084	0.530	1.240	0.371	1.068	0.463	1.124	0.447
X40	0.803	0.186	0.661	0.166	0.909	0.407	0.872	0.482
X41	0.833	0.130	0.708	0.124	1.140	0.214	1.267	0.184
X42	0.983	0.881	0.960	0.843	1.131	0.136	1.253	0.109

Table 5. (continued)

Variable	Dependent variable Y1				Dependent variable Y2			
	Ordered probit		Ordered logit		Ordered probit		Ordered logit	
	Odds ratio	Prob.	Odds ratio	Prob.	Odds ratio	Prob.	Odds ratio	Prob.
X43	0.761	0.166	0.591	0.145	1.503*	0.001	2.024*	0.001
X44	1.817*	0.001	3.179*	0.001	0.839***	0.102	0.741***	0.098
Climatic factors								
X45	0.866	0.311	0.797	0.385	0.844***	0.098	0.747***	0.094
X46	0.688	0.152	0.465	0.126	0.489*	0.000	0.303*	0.000
X47	0.868	0.338	0.752	0.297	0.847	0.137	0.757	0.142
X48	1.308	0.221	1.450	0.344	1.631*	0.001	2.269*	0.001
X49	0.981	0.924	1.104	0.794	0.806	0.153	0.695	0.160
X50	1.061	0.722	1.046	0.888	0.980	0.873	0.979	0.919
X51	0.946	0.682	0.899	0.675	1.059	0.565	1.129	0.487
X52	1.060	0.648	1.150	0.537	0.996	0.968	0.983	0.917
X53	1.003	0.983	1.035	0.888	1.114	0.303	1.195	0.313
X54	0.906	0.471	0.840	0.498	0.906	0.325	0.855	0.366
X55	1.212	0.213	1.483	0.154	1.061	0.626	1.109	0.616
X56	0.857	0.344	0.757	0.337	1.055	0.665	1.075	0.728
X57	0.985	0.926	0.972	0.921	0.935	0.591	0.892	0.595
X58	0.564*	0.002	0.329*	0.001	0.832	0.150	0.718	0.132
X59	1.358	0.100	1.690	0.114	1.032	0.823	1.073	0.770
X60	1.357**	0.046	1.828**	0.035	1.210	0.104	1.403***	0.099
X61	0.811	0.153	0.680	0.147	0.876	0.218	0.787	0.192
X62	0.802	0.152	0.692	0.192	0.837	0.104	0.731***	0.091
X63	0.889	0.331	0.801	0.305	1.113	0.266	1.189	0.291
Pseudo R-squared	0.350		0.354		0.306		0.305	
Prob (LR statistic)	<0.0000001		<0.0000001		<0.0000001		<0.0000001	
Sample size	460		460		460		460	

Note: *, **, *** indicates significant at 1%, 5%, 10% significance level, respectively.

In terms of odds ratios, results from the availability of food at household (Y1) logit model indicates that holding other things constant, for a unit increase in the common resources dependency for cattle or livestock feeding (X30), the odds in favour of availability of food at household (Y1) increases by 1.823, or about 82.3 per cent. Similarly, there is a 160.2 per cent increase of odds of availability of food for the household (Y1) for a one-unit increase in knowledge about taking precaution against dengue, malaria (X17). The odds of household food availability (Y1) for a household buying bulk amount of food (X12) is 304.6 per cent higher than the odds of household food availability (Y1) for a household without buying a bulk amount of food. For a unit increase in the earning ratio (X6), the odds in favour of availability of food at household (Y1) increases by 1.412 or about 41.2 per cent.

Holding other things constant, a unit increase in climatic issues affecting the kitchen environment (X58) increases the odds in favour of unavailability of food in the household (Y1) by (1-0.329), or about 67.1 per cent. Similarly, there is a 33.8 per cent increase of odds of unavailability of food at the household (Y1) for a one-unit increase in competition for common resources (X31). For a unit increase in poverty level or decrease of household poverty/economic status (X3), the odds in favour of unavailability of food at a household (Y1) increases by (1-0.59), or about 41 per cent. Similarly, there is a 47.2 per cent increase of odds of unavailability of food at household (Y1) for a one-unit increase in number of school going children (X2).

Results for household status of food accessibility (Y2) models show that, among the climatic factors, natural disasters at the local level (X45), and climatic impact on income (X46), climatic impact on household food storage system (X48), climatic impact on household sanitation system (X60), and climatic impact on increases of short term food prices (X62) are statistically significant. Among the non-climatic/general factors, prices of general food items (X22), the difference between rural and city food prices (X23), low level of income (X26), incidences of mosquitoes, insects, pest (X43), incidences of disease (X44), household transportation (X11), household poverty/economic status (X3), earning ratio (X6), spouse doing job (X4), and number of school going children (X2) are statistically significant. According to the probit model, households having savings (X7) also show a statistically significant relationship with household status of food accessibility.

With reference to the food accessibility at household (Y2) logit model, the odds ratio indicate that holding other things constant, for a unit increase in climatic impact on household food storage system (X48), the odds in favour of food security at the household (Y2) increases by 2.269 or about 126.9 per cent. Similarly, there is an 80 per cent increase of odds of food accessibility at household (Y2) for a one-unit increase in earning ratio (X6). The odds of household food accessibility (Y2) for household having transportation (X11) is 176.9 per cent higher than the odds of household without having transportation. The odds of household accessibility (Y2) for spouse being employed (X4) is 319.1 per cent higher than the odds of household without spouse doing job. The odds of household food accessibility (Y2) for household have savings (X7) is 48.9 per cent higher than the odds of household without having savings.

For this model, the odds on climatic factors indicate that holding other things constant, for a unit increase in natural disasters at the local level (X45), the odds in favour of food accessibility at a household (Y2) decreases by (1-0.747) or about 25.3 per cent. Similarly, there is a 69.7 per cent decrease of odds of food accessibility at household (Y2) for a one-unit increase in climatic impact on income (X46). For a unit increase in climatic impact on increases of short-time food prices (X62), the odds in favour of food accessibility at a household (Y2) decreases by (1-0.731), or about 26.9 per cent. Similarly, there is a 33.7 per cent decrease of odds of food accessibility at a household (Y2) for a one-unit increase in prices of general food items (X22). For a unit increase in difference between rural and city food prices (X23), the odds in favour of food accessibility at a household (Y2) decreases by (1-0.63) or about 37 per cent. Similarly, there is a 31.8 per cent decrease of odds of food accessibility at a household (Y2) for a one-unit increase in low level of income (X26). For a unit increase in incidences of disease (X44), the odds in favour of food accessibility at a household (Y2) decreases by (1-0.741) or about 25.9 per cent. Similarly, there is a 28.1 per cent decrease of odds of food accessibility at a household (Y2) for a one-unit increase in household poverty/economic status (X3). For a unit increase in number of school going children (X2), the odds in favour of food accessibility at household (Y2) decreases by (1-0.486) or about 51.4 per cent.

However, in the model, some of the variables show unexpected signs with respect to their relationship with household food security, such as the climatic impacts on sanitation system (X60), and the incidences of disease (X44) show the odds in favour of availability of food at a household (Y1). Similarly, the climatic impact on household sanitation system (X60) and incidences of, for example of mosquitoes, insects and pests (X43), show the odds in favour of food accessibility at a household (Y2). Therefore, new additional studies need to be undertaken to justify the unusual behaviour of these few variables.

Model efficiency test

To test the presence of multicollinearity among the variables, the Pearson Correlation tests have been performed in the study. When two variables are considered highly correlated to each other in explaining the dependent variable, it may give rise to multicollinearity problem. In the case of multicollinearity, the correlation value is considered as 0.8 or above (Field, 2000, pp. 2, 44-322). The result shows that the correlation values among the variables fall below 0.8, which indicates that multicollinearity problem is absent among the variables.

Moreover, logically this study is free from endogeneity (including causality) problem because in the survey, questions were asked about the impact of different factors on food security and not vice versa. Moreover, technically the *ordered dependent regression* or *ordinal regression* is based on the "Generalized Linear Models" (used by EViews statistical package) and "Generalized structural equation model" (used by Stata statistical package) in which the software itself takes some instrumental variables to solve the endogeneity problems.

IV. CONCLUSIONS AND POLICY RECOMMENDATIONS

The study finds that several resilience factors, climatic factors, and non-climatic factors are statistically significant to explain the household status of food security. It also finds that these factors differ between food secure and insecure groups.

Climate change is a major potential threat to household food security in Malaysia (Alam, Siwar and Al Amin, 2010; Alam and others, 2011). Therefore, to ensure sustainable household food security in the country, climate change must be integrated into the design of the Malaysian food security programmes. In addition, food security approaches must recognize climate change as an important driver. This integration would increase household capacity to adapt to climatic change. At the same time, climate change adaptation approaches and strategies to reduce vulnerability to climate change would also increase household food security.

Prioritization of needs for investment targeted at increasing food security adaptation to climate change is important. Climate change adaptations are concentrated on improving the potential of people, especially the most vulnerable groups, towards adapting to climate change. This involves extending support for livelihoods that are climate-resilient, reducing on disaster risk, advocacy, empowerment and social mobilization to curb the underlying causes of vulnerability (Alam and others, 2012b). To adequately deal with the effects of climate change on food security, plans have to be chalked out with a good analysis of the groups that are particularly marginal, as they are likely to be the most affected by climate change and have very limited capacities to cope with it.

Climate change affects groups that have always been at risk of food insecurity, but it also affects new groups who have become vulnerable to regional weather-changing conditions (IPCC, 2007). Most vulnerable groups have already practiced some form of risk management, but their capability to adapt to climatic change is often limited due to their extremely restricted coping-up potential. Thus, the climate change adaptation techniques and food security should empower the groups that are socially excluded to lower their vulnerability and improve their resilience (Stern, 2007; Pielke and others, 2007; Thompson and Metz, 1997). Work on adaptation must address food security as a major challenge faced by the populations that are vulnerable to climate, while food security plans, in most cases, give people the capability to adapt to changes in climate, specifically when climate change is taken explicitly into consideration.

Mitigation options are important when planning for the long term. People who are vulnerable should be empowered and encouraged to adapt to climate change by developing resilience through investments in health, social protection, education, infrastructure, and other methods. Monitoring weather extremes and design strategies for disaster preparation is also very important. Given these effects and the resources needed to adapt them, resources applied towards realizing the Sustainable Development Goals might be integrated into mitigation programmes of climatic change. Furthermore, the private sector should advocate mitigation methods, such as energy efficiency, renewable energy, developments and infrastructure, which includes, for example, dams, flood-resistant storage facilities, cyclone shelters and techniques for lowering water loss in distribution systems.

Finally, local, national, and regional administrations must be provided with sufficient resources to deal with the challenges of climate change. They should concentrate on the building of capacity in communities that are particularly at risk of food insecurity, as well as climatic changes. New studies should also be undertaken to validate or reject the overall findings of this study. The findings of the study are empirically very new. Therefore, there is a scope to explore this issue further. The results of this study can be investigated further and validated against other socioeconomic factors, demographic factors, different locations, different economic groups, and different measurements of the level of food security.

REFERENCES

Abdulai, Awudu, and Anna CroleRees (2001). Constraints to income diversification strategies: evidence from Southern Mali. *Food Policy*, vol. 26, No. 4, pp. 437-452.

Alam, Md. Mahmudul, Chamhur Siwar, and Abul Quasem Al-Amin (2010). Climate change adaptation policy guidelines for agricultural sector in Malaysia. *Asian Journal of Environmental and Disaster Management*, vol. 2, No. 4, pp. 463-469.

Alam, Md. Mahmudul, and others (2011). Farm level assessment of climate change, agriculture and food security issues in Malaysia. *World Applied Sciences Journal*, vol. 14, No. 3, pp. 431-442.

_____ (2012a). Initiatives and challenges of agricultural crop sector in ECER Development Projects in Malaysia. *American-Eurasian Journal of Agricultural & Environmental Science*, vol. 12, No. 7, pp. 922-931.

_____ (2012b). Paddy farmers' adaptation practices to climatic vulnerabilities in Malaysia. *Mitigation and Adaptation Strategies for Global Change*, vol. 17, No. 4, pp. 415-423.

_____ (2014). Impacts of climatic changes on paddy production in Malaysia: micro study on IADA at North West Selangor. *Research Journal of Environmental and Earth Sciences,* vol. 6, No. 5, pp. 251-258.

_____ (2016a). Climate change and food security of the Malaysian East Coast poor: a path modeling approach. *Journal of Economic Studies*, vol. 43, No. 3, pp. 458-474.

_____ (2016b). Food security and low-income households in the Malaysian East Coast Economic Region: an empirical analysis. *Review of Urban & Regional Development Studies,* vol. 28, No. 1, pp. 2-15.

Ali, R., and A.K. Ali (2009). Estimating the prospective impacts of global warming on Malaysian agriculture. Proceeding of 2nd National Conference on Agro-Environment 2009, MARDI. Malaysia, 24-26 March.

Arshad, F.M., M.N. Shamsudin, and R. Saleh (1999). Food security in Malaysia. Presented at Seminar on International Trade and Food Security. Asian Productivity Organization, Tokyo.

Baker, J.T., and L.H. Allen, Jr. (1993). Contrasting crop species responses to CO2 and temperature: rice, soybean and citrus. *Vegetatio*, vol. 104, No. 1, pp. 239-260.

Checkley, William, and others (2000). Effects of El Niño and ambient temperature on hospital admissions for diarrhoeal diseases in Peruvian children. *The Lancet,* vol. 355, pp. 442-450.

Cline, William R. (2007). *Global Warming and Agriculture: Impact Estimates by Country.* Washington, D.C.: Center for Global Development and Peterson Institute for International Economics.

Coates, Jennifer, Anne Swindale, and Paula Bilinsky (2007). *Household Food Insecurity Access Scale (HFIAS) for Measurement of Household Food Access: Indicator Guide*, vol. 3. Washington, D.C.: Food and Nutrition Technical Assistance Project, Academy for Educational Development.

Cristofar, Sharron P., and P. Peter Basiotis (1992). Dietary intakes and selected characteristics of women ages 19-50 years and their children ages 1-5 years by reported perception of food sufficiency. *Journal of Nutrition Education,* vol. 24, No. 2, pp. 53-58.

Cruz, Rex Victor, and others (2007). Asia. In *Climate Change 2007: Impacts, Adaptation and Vulnerability. Contribution of Working Group II to the Fourth Assessment Report of the Intergovernmental Panel on Climate Change*, M.L. Parry and others, eds., Cambridge, U.K.: Cambridge University Press.

Economic Commission for Africa (ECA) (2004). *Land Tenure Systems and Their Impacts on Food Security and Sustainable Development in Africa*. Addis Ababa.

East Coast Economic Region Development Council (ECERDC) (2007). ECER Master Plan: economic drivers of the region – agriculture. Malaysia.

_____ (2008). ECER Master Plan: success factors. Available from www.ecerdc.com.my/en/master-plan/success-factors/. Accessed 18 July 2016.

Energy Information Administration (EIA) (2005). *International Energy Annual 2005 – CO2 World Carbon Dioxide Emissions from the Consumption of Coal, 1980-2006 (Million Metric Tons of Carbon Dioxide)*. Washington, D.C.: Government of the United States.

Food and Agriculture Organization (FAO) (2003). *Trade Reforms and Food Security: Conceptualizing the Linkages*. Rome.

_____ (2005). *The State of Food Insecurity in the World 2005*. Rome.

_____ (2007). High prices and volatility in agricultural commodities. *Food Outlook*, November. Available from www.fao.org/docrep/010/ah876e/ah876e13.htm#21.

_____ (2008). Climate change and food security: a framework document. Rome: FAO Interdepartmental Working Group on Climate Change.

Fartahun, Melaku, and others (2007). Women's involvement in household decision making and strengthening social capital are crucial factors for child survival in Ethiopia. *Acta Paediatrica*, vol. 96, No. 4, pp. 582-589.

Field, Andy (2000). *Discovering Statistics Using SPSS for Windows*. Thousand Oaks, California: Sage Publications.

Frankenberger, Timothy R. (1992). Indicators and data collection methods for assessing household food security. In *Household Food Security: Concepts, Indicators, and Measurements: a Technical Review*, Simon Maxwell and Timothy R. Frankenberger, eds. New York: UNICEF; Rome: IFAD.

Hindin, Michelle J. (2006). Women's input in household decision and their nutritional status in three resource-constrained settings. *Public Health Nutrition*, vol. 9, No. 4, pp. 485-493.

Intergovernmental Panel on Climate Change (IPCC) (2007). *Climate Change 2007 - Impacts, Adaptation and Vulnerability. Contribution of Working Group II to the Fourth Assessment Report of IPCC*. Cambridge, U.K.: Cambridge University Press.

Iram, Uzma, and Muhammad S. Butt (2004). Determinants of household food security: an empirical analysis for Pakistan. *International Journal of Social Economics*, vol. 31, No. 8, pp. 735-766.

Kovats, R.S., and others (2004). The effect of temperature on food poisoning: time series analysis in 10 European countries. *Epidemiology and Infection*, vol. 132, No. 3, pp. 443-453.

Kundzewicz, Zbigniew W., and others (2007). Freshwater resources and their management. In *Climate Change 2007: Impacts, Adaptation and Vulnerability. Contribution of Working Group II to the Fourth Assessment Report of the Intergovernmental Panel on Climate Change*, Martin L. Parry and others, eds. Cambridge, U.K.: Cambridge University Press.

Lovendal, Christian Romer, and Macro Knowles (2006). Tomorrow's hunger: a framework for analysing vulnerability to food security. Research Paper, No. 2006/119. Helsinki: United Nations University – World Institute for Development Economic Research.

Mimura, Nobuo, and others (2007). Small islands. In *Climate Change 2007: Impacts, Adaptation and Vulnerability. Contribution of Working Group II to the Fourth Assessment Report of the Intergovernmental Panel on Climate Change*, Martin L. Parry and others, eds. Cambridge, U.K.: Cambridge University Press.

Ministry of Science, Technology and the Environment (MOSTE) (2001). *National Response Strategies to Climate Change.* Putrajaya, Malaysia.

Myntti, Cynthia (1993). Social determinants of child health in Yemen. *Social Science & Medicine*, vol. 37, No. 2, pp. 233-240.

National Hydraulic Research Institute of Malaysia (NAHRIM) (2006). *Final Report: Study of the Impact of Climate Change on the Hydrologic Regime and Water Resources of Peninsular Malaysia.* National Hydraulic Research Institute of Malaysia (NAHRIM) and California Hydrologic Research Laboratory (CHRL), Malaysia.

Negatu, Workneh. (2006). Determinants of small farm household food security: evidence from south Wollo, Ethiopia. *Ethiopian Journal of Development Research,* vol. 28, No. 1, pp.1-29.

Nyariki, Dickson M., and Steve Wiggins (1997). Household food insecurity in Sub-Saharan Africa: lesson from Kenya. *British Food Journal,* vol. 99, No. 7, pp. 249-262.

Olson, Christine M., and others (1997). Factors contributing to household food insecurity in rural upstate New York. *Family Economics and Nutrition Review*, vol. 10, pp. 2-17.

Pfeiffer, James, Stephen Gloyd, and Lucy Ramirez Li (2001). Intra-household resource allocation and child growth in Mozambique: an ethnographic case-control study. *Social Science & Medicine*, vol. 53, No. 1, pp. 83-97.

Piaseu, Noppawan (2006). Factors affecting food insecurity among urban poor in Thailand. *South African Journal of Clinical Nutrition*, vol. 18, pp. 156-161.

Pielke, Roger, and others (2007). Lifting the taboo on adaptation. *Nature,* vol. 445, No. 7128, pp. 597-598.

Rose, Donald, and Peter P. Basiotis (1995). Improving federal efforts to assess hunger and food insecurity. *FoodReview*, vol. 18, No. 1 (Jan-Apr), pp. 18-23.

Singh, S., and others (1996). Simulated impact of climate change on rice production in Peninsular Malaysia. *Proceeding of National Conference on Climate Change*. UPM, Malaysia.

Stern, Nicholas (2007). *The Economics of Climate Change: the Stern Review*. Cambridge, U.K.: Cambridge University Press.

Tashiro, Toru, and Ian F. Wardlaw (1989). A comparison of the effect of high temperature on grain development in wheat and rice. *Annals of Botany*, vol. 64, No. 1, pp. 59-65.

Thompson, Anne, and Manfred Metz (1997). *Implications of Economic Policy for Food Security: A Training Manual.* Training Materials for Agricultural Planning, 40. Rome: FAO.

_____(1998). *Implications of Economic Policy for Food Security: A Training Manual*. Rome. FAO and the German Agency for Technical Cooperation (GTZ).

Tisdell, Clem (1996). Economic indicators to assess the sustainability of conservation farming projects: an evaluation. *Agriculture, Ecosystems and Environment*, vol. 57, No. 2-3, pp. 117-131.

von Braun, Joachim. (2007). The world food situation: new driving forces and required actions. *Food Policy Report*. Washington, D.C.: International food Policy Research Institute.

Yamane, Taro (1967). *Statistics: An Introductory Analysis,* edition 2. New York: Harper and Row; Tokyo: John Weatherhill.

Zimmerman, M., and others (2007). Variability of total and Pathogenic Vibrio Parahaemolyticus Densities in Northern Gulf of Mexico water and oysters. *Applied and Environmental Microbiology,* vol. 73, No. 23, pp. 7589-7596.

APPENDIX

List of the variables

Y1   Household food availability in the last one month, where available enough of the kinds of food you want to eat = 1, others = 0

Y2   Household status of food accessibility, where food secure access = 1, others = 0

X1   Education level, where illiterate = 1, primary = 2, secondary = 3, certificate = 4

X2   Number of school going children, where no school going children = 1, 1-2 children = 2, 3 children = 3, 4-5 children = 4, more than 5 children = 5

X3   Household poverty/economic status, where marginally non-poor = 1, recently marginally non-poor = 2, poor = 3, hard core poor = 4

X4   Spouse doing job, where yes = 1, no = 0

X5   Head of household having supplementary job, where yes = 1, no = 0

X6   Earning ratio (earning family member/total family member) is coded in 1-5 scale based on equal value for every 20% ratio value, where 0-20%, 21-40%, 41-60%, 61-80%, and 81-100% are coded as 1, 2, 3, 4, 5, respectively

X7   Household having any savings, where yes = 1, no = 0

X8   Locality, where urban = 1, rural = 0

X9   Ownership of house, where yes = 1, no = 0

X10   Type of home, where wood made = 1, mixed = 2, brick = 3

X11   Household having any transport for buying food, where yes = 1, no = 0

X12   Household buying bulk amount of food, where yes = 1, no = 0

X13   Household having neat and clean kitchen and dining place, where yes = 1, no = 0

X14   Household having a hygienic sanitation facility, where strongly disagree = 1, disagree = 2, not sure = 3, agree = 4, strongly agree = 5

X15   Household managing waste properly, where strongly disagree = 1, disagree = 2, not sure = 3, agree = 4, strongly agree = 5

X16   Household having knowledge about maintaining nutritious and hygienic way of cooking and washing food, where strongly disagree = 1, disagree = 2, not sure = 3, agree = 4, strongly agree = 5

X17   Household having knowledge about taking precaution against dengue, malaria, etc., where strongly disagree = 1, disagree = 2, not sure = 3, agree = 4, strongly agree = 5

X18   The effectiveness of current food distribution process in Malaysia, where very low = 1, low = 2, normal = 3, high = 4, very high = 5

X19   Current road and transportation facility for food distribution process in Malaysia, where very low = 1, low = 2, normal = 3, high = 4, very high = 5

X20   Availability of expected food in the local market, where very low = 1, low = 2, normal = 3, high = 4, very high = 5

X21   Sufficiency of expected food in the local market, where very low = 1, low = 2, normal = 3, high = 4, very high = 5

X22   Current prices of general food items, where very low = 1, low = 2, normal = 3, high = 4, very high = 5

X23   Current difference between rural and city food prices, where very low = 1, low = 2, normal = 3, high = 4, very high = 5

X24   High prices of food cause household food shortage, where very low = 1, low = 2, normal = 3, high = 4, very high = 5

X25   Current level of household income, where very low = 1, low = 2, normal = 3, high = 4, very high = 5

X26   Low level of income cause household food shortage, where very low = 1, low = 2, normal = 3, high = 4, very high = 5

X27   Ready budget arrangement to buy food anytime, where very low = 1, low = 2, normal = 3, high = 4, very high = 5

X28   Availability of discount or offer on food price in the local market, where very low = 1, low = 2, normal = 3, high = 4, very high = 5

X29   The effectiveness of current food distribution process in Malaysia, where very low = 1, low = 2, normal = 3, high = 4, very high = 5

X30   Dependency on common resources for cattle or livestock feeding, where very low = 1, low = 2, normal = 3, high = 4, very high = 5

X31   Current competition among people for common resources, where very low = 1, low = 2, normal = 3, high = 4, very high = 5

X32   Current expenditure for feeding and medicine of cattle and livestock, where very low = 1, low = 2, normal = 3, high = 4, very high = 5

X33   Difference between rural and city food quality, where very low = 1, low = 2, normal = 3, high = 4, very high = 5

X34   Food quality or nutrition level in local market, where very low = 1, low = 2, normal = 3, high = 4, very high = 5

X35   Food quality on food safety in local market, where very low = 1, low = 2, normal = 3, high = 4, very high = 5

X36   Quality of drinking water, where very low = 1, low = 2, normal = 3, high = 4, very high = 5

X37   Stability of food price, where very low = 1, low = 2, normal = 3, high = 4, very high = 5

X38   Price variation among shops in the local market, where very low = 1, low = 2, normal = 3, high = 4, very high = 5

X39   Access of quick credit to buy food, where very low = 1, low = 2, normal = 3, high = 4, very high = 5

X40   Stability of food supply, where very low = 1, low = 2, normal = 3, high = 4, very high = 5

X41   Unavailability of food in market leading food shortage, where very low = 1, low = 2, normal = 3, high = 4, very high = 5

X42   Agencies support for household food security, where very low = 1, low = 2, normal = 3, high = 4, very high = 5

X43   Current level of incidences of mosquitos, insects, pest, etc., where very low = 1, low = 2, normal = 3, high = 4, very high = 5

X44   Current level of incidences of disease like dengue, malaria, heat stretch, cold, skin disease, etc., where very low = 1, low = 2, normal = 3, high = 4, very high = 5

X45   Occurrences of natural disasters such as flood, cyclone, landslides, etc. at local level, where very low = 1, low = 2, normal = 3, high = 4, very high = 5

X46   Climatic issues and related disease reduce income, where yes = 1, no = 0

X47   Climatic issues affect household food collection system, where strongly disagree = 1, disagree = 2, not sure = 3, agree = 4, strongly agree = 5

X48   Climatic issues affect household food storage system (e.g. refrigerator, packaging), where strongly disagree = 1, disagree = 2, not sure = 3, agree = 4, strongly agree = 5

X49   Climatic issues affect household food storage process (e.g. dry, salty, oily), where strongly disagree = 1, disagree = 2, not sure = 3, agree = 4, strongly agree = 5

X50   Climatic issues increase household food storage cost, where strongly disagree = 1, disagree = 2, not sure = 3, agree = 4, strongly agree = 5

X51   Climatic issues affect household usage or utilization of land, where strongly disagree = 1, disagree = 2, not sure = 3, agree = 4, strongly agree = 5

X52   Climatic issues reduce normal food test, where strongly disagree = 1, disagree = 2, not sure = 3, agree = 4, strongly agree = 5

X53   Climatic issues reduce food longevity, where strongly disagree = 1, disagree = 2, not sure = 3, agree = 4, strongly agree = 5

X54   Climatic issues affect household food choice and habit, where strongly disagree = 1, disagree = 2, not sure = 3, agree = 4, strongly agree = 5

X55   Climatic issues affect household cooking system (e.g. cooking by gas or stove not by woods), where strongly disagree = 1, disagree = 2, not sure = 3, agree = 4, strongly agree = 5

X56   Climatic issues affect cooking time and amount (e.g. large amount of cooking together or several time cooking for hot food or several times heating for not rotating), where strongly disagree = 1, disagree = 2, not sure = 3, agree = 4, strongly agree = 5

X57   Climatic issues cause to eat outside or buy ready food from outside, where strongly disagree = 1, disagree = 2, not sure = 3, agree = 4, strongly agree = 5

X58   Climatic issues affect the environment and cleanness of kitchen, where strongly disagree = 1, disagree = 2, not sure = 3, agree = 4, strongly agree = 5

X59   Climatic issues affect household waste management, where strongly disagree = 1, disagree = 2, not sure = 3, agree = 4, strongly agree = 5

X60   Climatic issues affect home sanitation system, where strongly disagree = 1, disagree = 2, not sure = 3, agree = 4, strongly agree = 5

X61   Climatic issues hamper food aid services and food supports programme, where strongly disagree = 1, disagree = 2, not sure = 3, agree = 4, strongly agree = 5

X62   Climatic issues increase short term food prices, where strongly disagree = 1, disagree = 2, not sure = 3, agree = 4, strongly agree = 5

X63   Climatic issues cause to increase food price in restaurant, where strongly disagree = 1, disagree = 2, not sure = 3, agree = 4, strongly agree = 5

IMPACT OF POPULATION ON CARBON EMISSION: LESSONS FROM INDIA

Chandrima Sikdar and Kakali Mukhopadhyay*

The global population is more than seven billion and will likely reach nine billion by 2050. As India is home to 18 per cent of the world's population, but has only 2.4 per cent of the land area, a great deal of pressure is being placed on all of the country's natural resources. The increasing population has been trending towards an alarming situation; the United Nations has estimated that the country's population will increase to 1.8 billion by the 2050 and, by 2028, it will overtake China as the world's most populous country. The growing population and the environmental deterioration are becoming major impediments in the country's drive to achieve sustained development in the country.

In this backdrop, the present study develops an econometric model to explain the causal relationship between carbon dioxide (CO_2) emission and population, given the population structure, industrial structure and economic growth in India. Based on this modelling exercise, the paper estimates the energy consumption and generation of CO_2 emission in 2050. The study projects that the total CO_2 emission in India will be 3.5 million metric tons in 2050.

JEL classification: J11, Q5, Q54.

Keywords: CO2 emission, population, population structure, India, STIRPAT model.

*   Chandrima Sikdar, corresponding author, Associate Professor, School of Business Management, Narsee Monjee Institute of Management Studies, Mumbai – 400056, India (e-mail: chandrimas4 @gmail.com, chandrima.sikdar@nmims.edu); and Kakali Mukhopadhyay, Senior Associate Fellow, Department of Natural Resource Sciences, Agricultural Economics Program, McGill University, Macdonald Campus, 21,111 Lakeshore Road, Ste. Anne de Bellevue, Montreal, Quebec, Canada-H9X3V9 (Tel: 1 5143988651, fax: 1 5143987990, e-mail: kakali.mukhopadhyay@mcgill.ca).

I. INTRODUCTION

Research and interest on population dynamics and environmental change was given renewed impetus by the United Nations Conference on Environment and Development in its Agenda 21, which was adopted in Rio de Janeiro, Brazil, in 1992. In Agenda 21, the development and dissemination of knowledge on the links between demographic trends and sustainable development, including environmental impacts, was recommended (United Nations, 1993).

The global population exceeds seven billion and is expected to reach nine billion by 2050. According to recent United Nations estimates, the global population is increasing by approximately 80 million — the size of Germany — each year. India is home to 18 per cent of the world's population, but it has only 2.4 per cent of the total land. Based on this, pressure on the countries resources is expected to persist.[1] The increase in population in India has been trending towards an alarming situation. According to the United Nations, the population of India will increase to 1.8 billion by 2050, which would make the country the most populous country in the world ahead of China.

The world's energy consumption is forecast to increase by 37 per cent during the next two decades, amid the rising global population and growing demand from Asian markets. While renewables will account for 8 per cent of the energy mix, up from its current level of 3 per cent, and fossil fuels will continue to meet two thirds of the increase in energy demand, according to the benchmark study. However, continued demand for fossil fuels means the world will not be able to reduce greenhouse gases in the atmosphere to about 450 parts per million of CO_2, which is the so-called 450 Scenario and seen as crucial for capping the rise in global temperature by 2°C, as outlined by the International Energy Agency (IEA, 2007). CO_2 emissions from fossil fuel combustion and industrial processes contributed a major portion of total greenhouse gas emissions during the period 1970-2010.[2] CO_2 emissions are expected to be 18 billion tons above the IEA 450 Scenario by 2035

---

[1] Over the past century, population and economic production increased about twentyfold, along with the demand for natural resources.

[2] The Intergovernmental Panel on Climate Change (IPCC) in its recent report – the Fifth Assessment Report (AR5), published in 2014 — has observed that, there has been an increasing trend in the anthropogenic emissions of greenhouse gases since the advent of the industrial revolution, with about half of the anthropogenic carbon dioxide (CO_2) emissions during this period occurring in the last 40 years. The period 1983-2012 is likely to have been the warmest 30-year period of the last 1,400 years. The change in the climate system is likely to have adverse impacts on livelihoods, cropping pattern and food security. Extreme heat events are likely to be longer and more intense in addition to changes in the precipitation patterns. Adverse impacts are likely to be felt more acutely in tropical zone countries, such as India, and within India, the poor will be more exposed.

(BP Energy Outlook, 2015). Specifically, India is one of the most important transitional and growing economies in the world.[3] Over the last three decades, India has sustained impressive gross domestic product (GDP) growth, with an average rate of 5.4 per cent per year. This economic growth is likely to be associated with greater energy use and increased air pollution. Industrial growth in the country has, in terms of the long-run trend, remained aligned with the GDP growth rate. The long-term average annual growth of industries comprising mining, manufacturing, and electricity, during the post-reform period between 1991-1992 and 2011-2012, averaged 6.7 per cent as against GDP growth of 6.9 per cent. Inclusion of construction in industry raises this growth to 7.0 per cent. The share of industry, including construction, in GDP remained generally stable, at about 28 per cent, in the post-reform period. The share of manufacturing, which is the most dominant sector within industry, however, did not show an impressive increase. It remained around the 14-16 per cent range during this period.

The development of a diversified industrial structure in India based on a combination of large and small-scale industries and the growing populations in both urban and rural areas have put pressures on the environment, as reflected in the growing incidence of air, water, and land degradation. India is currently highly reliant on fossil fuels to meet its energy needs. The country's production of total primary energy, including coal and lignite, crude petroleum and natural gas, has increased from 3.1 quadrillion British thermal units (BTU) in 1980/81 to 15.9 quadrillion BTU in 2011/12, an increase of five times, while consumption increased almost seven times (figure 1). In 2007, coal and oil together accounted for two thirds of the primary energy, with the remainder being predominantly biomass and waste. To develop further, India requires reliable access to increasing supplies of energy.

Energy security is, therefore, a primary concern for India, but there are several reasons why attention has also turned to climate issues in recent years. One of them is that India is vulnerable to climate change, which could have a number of negative effects, such as decreased yields of wheat and rice (two of its major exports) and increased sea level and water stress. The main concern related to air pollution at present is greenhouse gas emissions,[4] owing to their role in contemporary global climate change. Greenhouse gas emissions, which are derived mainly from combustion and CO2 emission levels, have climbed quickly in the current century (figure 2). Industrial pollution is concentrated in such industries as petroleum

---

[3]   India is still poor by global standards, with a gross national income (GNI) per capita of about $5,350 (in PPP) in 2013, compared with $53,750 for the United States of America (World Bank, 2015).

[4]   The major greenhouse gas is carbon dioxide, released to the atmosphere mainly by fossil fuel burning (80 per cent), but also by burning of forests (20 per cent).

Figure 1. Energy consumption in India in quadrillion British thermal unit (1980-2012)

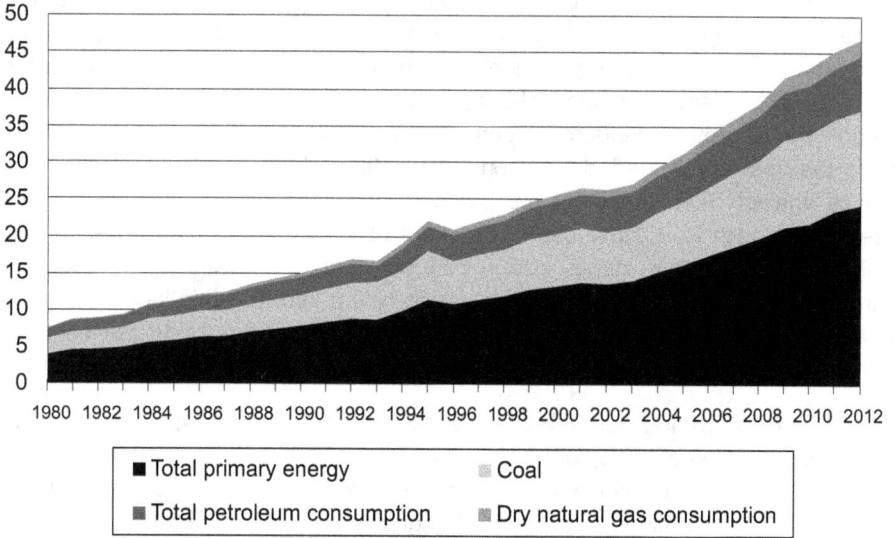

Source: EIA (2015).

Figure 2. Carbon dioxide emission from energy consumption in India (1980-2012) in million metric tons

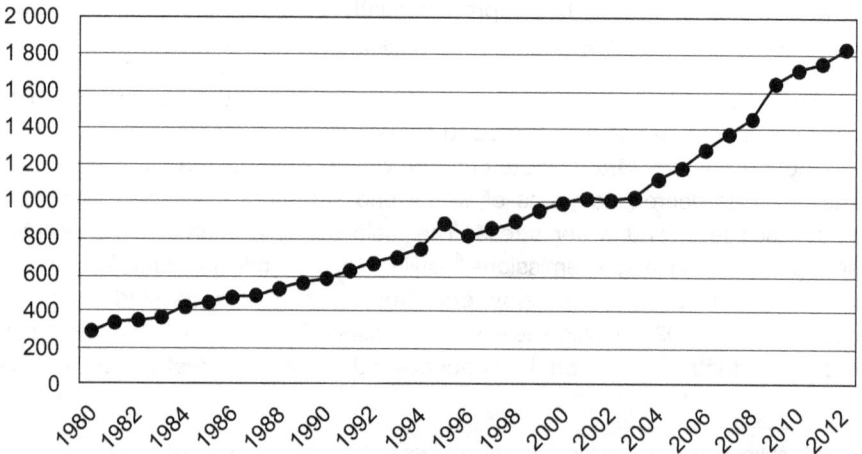

Source: EIA (2015).

refineries, textiles, pulp and paper, industrial chemicals, iron and steel, and non-metallic mineral products. Small-scale industries, especially foundries, chemical manufacturing, and brick making, are also significant polluters. In the power sector, thermal power, which constitutes the bulk of installed capacity for electricity generation, is a significant source of air pollution. As long as smokestack, chimney, and tailpipe emissions are unregulated, or ineffectively regulated, and as long as technological change does not fundamentally affect pollution levels, population remains a crucial variable for such countries as India. Therefore, policies and investment must encourage more efficient use of resources, the substitution of scarce resources and the adoption of technologies and practices that minimize environmental impact. Fortunately, the Government of India has already made some positive moves in this direction.

Thus, the major challenge for India with regard to controlling carbon emission levels is its population growth. This is because the country's population is projected to increase to a level that will lead to an overall scarcity of resources, which will, in turn, result in greater fossil fuel combustion and also carbon emissions. A general question that arises from this is: What would be the impact of this population growth on the carbon emission levels in India? To answer this question, the present paper uses a STIRPAT model, a framework widely used in literature to study the environmental impacts of population and affluence in an economy. However, to show a more complete and accurate impact of population change on carbon emission levels, along with GDP per capita, which is used as an indicator of affluence, the present paper incorporates two more variables in the STIRPAT modelling framework: household size and industry value added in GDP. Using time series data for the Indian economy for the period 1980-2012, the impact of population change on carbon emissions is quantitatively assessed and analysed. Based on this analysis, the paper attempts to project the extent of carbon dioxide emission in India in 2050.

The organizational structure of the paper is as follows: section II presents a brief review of literature. Section III discusses the model. Section IV provides the data, the data sources and statistical testing of data. Section V elaborates the estimation technique to arrive at the estimated coefficients and provides the projection for carbon emissions in India during 2050. A detailed discussion of the results obtained is carried out in section VI. Section VII finally concludes the paper with a summary of the main findings and the policy implications.

II. LITERATURE REVIEW

As the effect of population on carbon emissions is wide ranging, identifying the relationship between them is a truly challenging exercise. In terms of population characteristics, key demographic factors, such as population size, its structure and distribution, are constantly changing, making the effect of these changes on carbon emission extremely complicated and varied. Researchers around the world have, thus, been much engaged in analysing the relationship between population growth and increasing carbon emission levels on one hand and analysing the impacts of changing population characteristics on emission levels on the other.

A large volume of literature has already contributed to this field. According to Birdsall (1992), population growth in developing countries results in large greenhouse gas emissions because of increased energy demand for power generation, industry, and transport, which, in turn, leads to increased fossil fuel consumption. However, he notes that a reduction in population growth matters, but is not the key factor in levelling off carbon emissions. Knapp and Mookerjee (1996) explore the nature of the relationship between global population growth and CO_2 emissions using the Granger causality test on annual data for the period 1880-1989, as well as more comprehensive error correction and cointegration models. The results suggest lack of a long-term equilibrium relationship, but imply a short-term dynamic relationship between CO_2 and population growth. Using decomposition analyses, Bongaarts (1992) shows that population growth is a key factor in greenhouse gas emissions growth.

The effect of changes in household size and urbanization on carbon emissions is another research focus. Dalton and others (2007) incorporate household size into the population-environment-technology model to stimulate economic growth, as well as changes in the consumption of various goods, direct and indirect energy demand, and carbon emissions over the next 100 years. Jiang and Hardee (2011) discuss the impact of shrinking household size on carbon emissions and argue that households, rather than individuals in a population, should be used as the variable in analysing demographic impact on emissions. This approach is favourable considering that households are the units of consumption, and possibly also the units of production in developing societies. Poumanyvong and Kaneko (2010) empirically investigate the effects of urbanization on energy use and CO_2 emissions. In the investigation, the authors consider different development stages using the STIRPAT model and a balanced panel dataset that covers the period 1975-2005 and includes 99 countries. The findings suggest that the impact of urbanization on carbon emissions is positive for all income groups, but that this effect is more pronounced in the middle-income group than in the other income groups. Barido and Marshal (2014) investigate empirically how national-level CO_2 emissions are affected by urbanization and environmental policy. They use statistical modelling to explore panel data on annual CO_2 emissions from 80 countries for the period 1983-2005. The results indicate that on the global average the urbanization-emission elasticity value is 0.95

(a 1 per cent increase in urbanization correlates with a 0.95 per cent increase in emissions). Several regions display a statistically significant, positive elasticity for fixed- and random-effects models: lower-income Europe, India and the subcontinent, Latin America, and Africa. Bekhet and Yasmin (2014) examine the causal relationship among economic growth, CO_2 emissions, energy consumption and urbanization in Malaysia for the period 1970-2012. The bounds F test yields evidence of a long-run relationship among per capita carbon emissions, per capita energy consumption, per capita real income, and urbanization. The results show that an increase in energy consumption results in an increase in per capita carbon emissions and urbanization in the long run. These results support the validity of the "Urban Transition Theory" developing stage in the Malaysian economy. This means that the level of CO_2 emissions is still increasing with the rapid urbanization process in Malaysia and that the expanding sprawl of the cities will harm the environment in the country in the long run in Malaysia.

A large number of studies analysed the impact of population and population structure on the environment, in particular on carbon emission using the IPAT/STIRPAT models. Shi (2003), using IPAT exercise, analyses CO_2 emissions in 93 countries between 1976 and 1995. He submits evidence that emission level rises disproportionately with population, the other variables in the model are GDP per capita, percentage of manufacturing in GDP, and percentage of population in the work force. He also finds that population elasticity of CO_2 is higher in developing than in developed countries. Fan and others (2006) analyse the impact of population, affluence, and technology on total CO_2 emissions of countries at different income levels at the global scale over the period 1975-2000. The results show that the working age population (15-64 years) has less of an effect on CO_2 emissions than do population size, affluence, and technology.

MacKellar and others (1995), covering the years 1970-1990 at the world scale, attribute roughly one third of CO_2 emissions to population, a percentage that more than doubles when population is represented by number of households rather than by individuals. Engelman (2010) similarly deduces from the simultaneous decrease of per capita emissions and increase of total emissions that the number of emitters must be a significant factor. Raskin (1995) suggests that from an environmental point of view, population stabilisation in wealthier countries should take priority over that in poorer countries. Satterthwaite (2009) negates the population factor after noting the low per capita greenhouse gas emissions of the world's two billion poorest people. Dalton and others (2008) incorporate population age structure into an energy-economic growth model with multiple dynasties of heterogeneous households to estimate and compare the effects of ageing populations and technical change on the baseline paths of United States energy use and CO_2 emissions. The authors show that an ageing population reduces long-term emissions by almost 40 per cent in a low-population scenario, and that the effects of the ageing process on emissions can be as large as, or larger than, those of technical change in some cases, given a closed economy, fixed substitution elasticity, and fixed labour supply over time.

Zhu and Peng (2012) examine the impacts of population size, population structure, and consumption level on carbon emissions in China from 1978 to 2008. Using a STIRPAT exercise, the study finds that changes in the consumption level and population structure are the two major factors that affect carbon emissions. Population size is not important. Regarding population structure, urbanization, population age and household size have distinct effects on carbon emissions. Urbanization increases carbon emissions, while the effect of age acts primarily through the expansion of the labour force and consequent overall economic growth. Households, rather than individuals, are a more reasonable explanation for the demographic impact on carbon emissions. Liddle (2014) summarizes the evidence from cross-country, macro-level studies that demographic factors and processes, specifically, population, age structure, household size, urbanization, and population density, influence carbon emissions and energy consumption. Higher population density is associated with lower levels of energy consumption and emissions.

Thus, while contemporary researchers around the world have extensively studied the impact of population growth on the environment, carbon emission levels, in particular, similar studies that focus on India are limited. Some of the recent studies on the Indian economy were conducted by Ghosh (2010); Martínez-Zarzoso and Maruotti (2011); Mukhopadhyay (2011); Ozturk and Salah Uddin (2012), and Yeo and others (2015).

Ghosh (2010) examines the carbon emissions and economic growth nexus for India. Using a multivariate cointegration approach, the study fails to establish a long-run equilibrium relationship and long-term causality between carbon emissions and economic growth; however, it establishes the existence of a bidirectional short-run causality between the two. Martínez-Zarzoso and Maruotti (2011) do a STIRPAT modelling to primarily analyse the impact of urbanization on CO_2 emissions involving a sample of ninety-five developing countries, of which India is one of them, from 1975 to 2003. India is classified as a low-income country in the study. Results of the study show that the emission-population elasticity is greater than one for all upper-, middle- and lower-income countries. However, the emission-urbanization elasticity is greater than unity for upper-income countries. For the other groups of countries, it is 0.72. Mukhopadhyay (2011) estimates the emissions of carbon dioxide, sulfur dioxide, and nitrogen oxide in India during the period 1983-1984 to 2006-2007. Using input-output structural decomposition analysis, he investigates the changes in emissions and the various factors responsible for those changes. He finds that industrial emissions of air pollutants have increased considerably in India during 1983-1984 to 2006-2007 with the main factors for these increases being changes in the final demand, changes in intensity and changes in technology. Ozturk and Salah Uddin (2012) study the long-run causality among carbon emission and energy consumption and growth in India and reports that there is feedback causal relationship between energy consumption and economic growth in India, which implies that the level of economic activity and energy consumption mutually influence each other; a high level of economic growth leads to a high level of energy consumption and vice versa.

Yeo and others (2015) identify and analyse the key drivers behind the changes of CO_2 emissions, particularly in the residential sectors of two emerging economies, namely India and China, during the period 1999-2011. Five socioeconomic factors, namely, energy emissions coefficients, energy consumption structure, energy intensity, household income and population size, are identified as the key factors driving the CO_2 emission levels in India. Using the logarithmic mean Divisia index (LMDI) method to decompose the changes in the emission levels, the study finds that from 1990 to 2011, the biggest contributor to the rise in emissions has been the increase in the country's per capita income level followed by the increasing population and changes in the energy consumption structure. The increases in emission levels brought about by these factors are 173 MtCO2e, 65.9 MtCO2e and 60.7 MtCO2e, respectively. On the other hand, changes in energy intensity followed by changes in the carbon emission coefficient have been the main factors behind lower carbon emission levels in the country during this period. While the energy intensity decreased the emission by 86.1 MtCO2e, the carbon emission coefficient lowered it by 14.4 MtCO2e. Thus, the stable economic growth and expansion experienced by the country during the two decades primarily resulted in increased energy demand and hence higher levels of CO_2 emission, while improved energy intensity by the way of investments for energy savings, technological improvements and energy efficiency policies were effective in mitigating CO_2 emissions in India.

These studies identify economic growth, rising income levels, population growth, urbanization and real investment as factors driving CO_2 emission levels in India. Some of the earlier works of Mukhopadhyay (2001; 2002), Mukhopadhyay and Chakraborty (2002; 2004), Gupta (1997) and Murthy, Panda and Parikh (1997) also point to similar such factors behind carbon emissions in India. In particular, they have found that economic growth and growing income levels have been the main contributing factors to emission levels over time.

The Intergovernmental Panel on Climate Change (IPCC) indicates that the key driving forces of CO_2 emissions in any economy are demographic changes, socioeconomic development and the rate and direction of technological change. As pointed out by different studies, in India, the key driving forces of CO_2 emissions are similar, namely economic growth, demographic profile, technological change, energy resource endowments, geographic integration of markets, institutions and policies (Shukla, 2006). Shukla (2006) constructs emission scenarios for India for the medium run (2000-2030) and the long run (2000-2100) based on the IPCC SRES[5] framework (IPCC, 2000) and finds that it is the endogenous development choices that will play a significant role in shaping the emission pathways in each of these scenarios. For both medium-run and long-run time periods, he predicts that the carbon emission trajectories in India under all of the scenarios are more or less linear, indicating a sustained rising emission trend throughout the century in all possible scenarios.

Thus, some researchers have focused on studying carbon emission levels in India and the factors that influence them while others have projected the trajectories for carbon emission in the country under different development scenarios for hundred years from 2000 to 2100. However, none of these studies look at population and population structure closely as the driving factors. With a population projection of 1.8 billion for the country by 2050, a careful study and understanding of the impact of this likely population growth on carbon emission levels is absolutely important, particularly in view of the country's pledge to support the Durban Platform for Enhanced Action to improve cooperation aimed at reaching a global agreement on climate change to be effective by 2020 (Gambhir and Anandarajah, 2013). The present study seeks to contribute to this research gap.

III. THE MODEL

STIRPAT modelling is a research framework for the stochastic estimation of the well-known IPAT identity model of environmental impact. The IPAT identity (Ehrlich and Holdren, 1971) is an equation that is usually used to analyse the impact of human behaviour on environmental pressures. It is given as:

$$I = PAT \tag{1}$$

Where I denotes environmental impact, P denotes population, A denotes affluence and T denotes technology.

Equation (1) is an accounting identity in which one term is derived from the value of the other three terms. The model requires data on only any of the three variables for one or some observational units and these can be used to measure only the constant proportional impacts of the independent variables on the dependent

---

[5]   SRES stands for Special Report on Emissions Scenarios.

variable. Thus, the multiplicative identity framework of IPAT is problematic for empirical analysis. Dietz and Rosa (1997) recognized this and reformulated the equation (1) into a stochastic model as under

$$I = a\, P^b\, A^c T^d \varepsilon \tag{2}$$

Where, I, P, A and T are the same as in IPAT equation (1); a, b, c and d are the coefficients and ε is the error term.

With this reformulation as in equation (2), the data on I, P, A and T can be used to estimate a, b, c, d and ε using the regression methods of statistics. Thus, with the reformulated version, the IPAT accounting model is converted into a general linear model, to which statistical methods can be applied and the non-proportionate importance of each influencing factor may be assessed.

Given in logarithmic form (York and others, 2003b) equation (2) is as under:

$$lnI = lna + b\,(lnP) + c\,(lnA) + d\,(lnT) + \varepsilon \tag{3}$$

Equation (3) presents an additive regression model in which all variables are in logarithmic forms. This natural logarithmic forms allow the terms to be estimated as elasticities (York and others, 2003b), where coefficients are given as percentage change. Thus, coefficients b, c and d in equation (3) are respectively the population, affluence and technology elasticities. Any coefficient closer to unity imply unit elasticity and represent proportional change in dependent variable due to change in independent variable; while coefficients greater than one denote more than a proportional change in the dependent variable brought about by a change in independent variables.

STIRPAT analysis usually begins with this basic framework and goes on to add or eliminate variables in an attempt to test different model specifications at different scales and regions. Total population size and GDP per capita are the most commonly used metrics in literature for P and A, while CO_2 emissions or similar derivative metrics, such as global warming potential (GWP) and CO_2 equivalents, are usual units used for I. Many studies eliminate "T" altogether and estimate only P and A and hence avoid the difficulty of operationalizing "T". According to York and others (2003a) and Wei (2011), "T" should be included in "ε", the error term and not treated separately in an application of the STIRPAT model. This is for consistency with the IPAT model where "T" is solved to balance I, P and A.

To capture the complete comprehensive impact of population changes in India on the country's carbon emission levels, the present paper proposes the STIRPAT model of the following form:

$$InI = Ina + b_{iva} (InI_{va}) + b_h (InAHHS) + b_A (InA) + \varepsilon \qquad (4)$$

Where, I denotes CO_2 emissions per capita (in million metric tons)

I_{va} denotes the share of industry value added as per cent of GDP

AHHS denotes the average household size

A denotes the GDP per capita

a denotes the constant

ε denotes the error term.

In equation (4), the impact (I) is measured as CO_2 emissions per capita while A is the usual affluence term of an IPAT identity. To this identity, the present study incorporates variables – I_{va} and AHHS.

With 18 per cent of the world's population on 2.4 per cent of its land area, India already is putting a great deal of pressure on all its natural resources. Furthermore, with the estimated increase in population, it is obvious that this pressure will increase manifold in years to come, leading to increased resource scarcity and fossil fuel combustion and hence higher levels of carbon emissions. Therefore, to understand a more comprehensive impact of the population growth, the present study uses emission per capita rather than total carbon emission as the dependent variable.

Average household size is an indicator of population structure. Given a fixed population size, a change in the number of households brought about by a change in average household size can influence the scale and structure of consumption in a large way and thereby significantly affect carbon emission levels. In addition, in an economic structure, such as in India, often households rather than individuals in the population are the units of energy consumption. Studies on relations between population structure and carbon emission levels have often used the working age population (15-64) as an indicator of population structure. However, such a broad age structure is likely to be related to total population. A more disaggregated age structure (Liddle and Lung, 2010; Liddle, 2011; Roberts, 2014) would probably reflect better the demographic impact on emissions, but because of the lack of available data on disaggregated age structure for India, average household size is used as a metric of population structure in the present study.

Industry value added in GDP is used as a metric for industrial structure. This is in line with the literature. As pointed out in section I, manufacturing, the most dominant area of the industrial sector, did not show much increase in its GDP share. In fact, the manufacturing value added of 16 per cent of the 1980s declined to

15.8 per cent in the 1990s and further to 15.3 per cent from 2000 and 2009 (World Development Indicators).[6] However, the long-run growth trend of Indian industries did stay aligned with the GDP growth rate. Moreover, the industrial structure has diversified into large and small-scale industries and have been reportedly putting pressures on the environment, as reflected in the growing incidence of air, water and land degradation. Furthermore, the Indian economy now is at a major turning point. With the current initiatives of the Government of India, such as Make in India[7] and Startup India,[8] the industrial sector is expected to emerge as a major sector. This, in turn, has its implications on energy use and consequent carbon emissions in the country.

IV. DATA AND STATISTICAL TESTS FOR DATA

The data required for the empirical implementation of the STIRPAT model are:

- Annual data for CO2 emissions (CO2) from energy consumption in metric tons per capita for India from 1980 to 2012 obtained from the World Development Indicators;

- Annual data for real GDP per capita (in millions) in India for the period 1980-2012, also obtained from the World Development Indicators;

- The industry valued added as per cent of GDP for India for the period 1980-2012, also obtained from the World Development Indicators;

- Average household size for India for the period, which is available from the Ministry of Statistics and Programme Implementation, Government of India.

Figure 3 presents the changing rates of all the variables of the model with 1980 as the base. As is observed, almost all the variables appear to be non-stationary with either a continuous uptrend or downtrend during the period. Of all the variables, carbon emission shows the most rapid growth rate, followed by GDP per capita, population and industry valued added. Average household size has shown negative

---

[6]   World Bank, World Development Indicators database. Available from http://data.worldbank.org/data-catalog/world-development-indicators (accessed 20 April 2015).

[7]   Make in India is an initiative of the Government of India to encourage multinationals and domestic companies to manufacture their products in India. This initiative was launched by Prime Minister Narendra Modi on 25 September 2014.

[8]   Startup India campaign is an initiative of the Government of India to boost entrepreneurship and encourage startups with job creation. It was launched by Prime Minister Narendra Modi on 16 January 2016.

Figure 3. Rate of change in carbon emission per capita, gross domestic product per capita, population, and population and industrial structure in India during the period 1980-2012

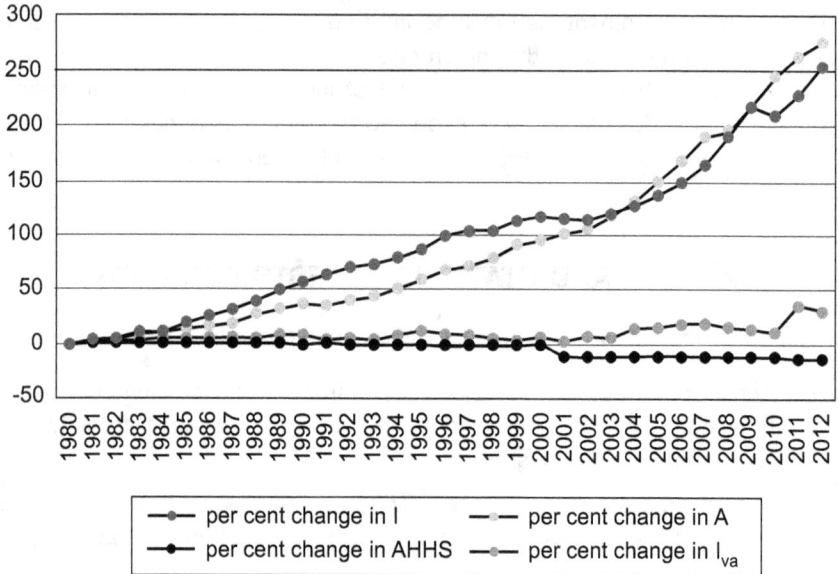

Source: Authors' calculation based on the data used in the model.

Note: AHHS, average household size.

growth during the time period. This non-stationarity of the variables needs to be taken care of to come up with precise and reliable estimates for the coefficients of the model.

Thus, the study of the causal relationship between carbon emissions and population changes in India involves the following steps:

Test for stationary

Test for stationary – estimation involving time series data set should be first checked for stationarity; without this initial test, the results of the regression can be highly misleading, as time series data may contain a trend element. A deterministic trend in estimation involving time series data may be taken care of by including a trend variable in the estimating model. But accounting for stochastic trend requires a more detailed exercise of conducting number of tests before proceeding with the estimation. In the absence of such tests, the estimation may be spurious.

Thus, an important econometric task is first to test if a time series data set is trending. If it is found to be trending, then some form of trend removal should be applied.

Trend in time series data is usually accounted by removing or de-trending the series. Two common de-trending procedures are first differencing and time trend regression. Unit root tests are used to determine if the trending data should be first differenced or regressed on deterministic functions of time so as to render the data stationary. Thus, unit root tests that consider the null hypothesis in which at least one unit root exists determines if the data are non-stationary against the alternative hypothesis that the series is stationary.

The most popular of those tests are the Augmented Dickey Fuller (ADF) and the Phillips-Perron (PP) unit root tests. The tests differ mainly on how they treat the serial correlation in the test regression. The test regression equation involving the series lnI is given as

$$\Delta lnI_t = \alpha + \beta t + \delta lnI_{t-1} + \sum_i^k \beta \, \Delta lnI_{t-i} + \varepsilon_t \tag{5}$$

Where, α is the constant, β is the coefficient of trend; δ is the coefficient of the lagged variable lnI_{t-1} and ε_t is the error term. k is the length of the lag and it makes the error a stochastic variable. The unit root tests of ADF and PP test the null hypothesis with two more formulations of the test regression equation – one where $\alpha = 0$ but $\beta \neq 0$ and the other where both $\alpha = 0$ and $\beta = 0$. The series lnI is considered stationary if any one of the three formulations of the test regression equation rejects the null hypothesis H0: $\delta = 0$, i.e. the series has at least one unit root.

The results of the unit root tests for the variables of model (as in equation 4) are presented in table 1.

The ADF and PP results (refer to column 8 of table 1) indicate that all the variables – CO2 emissions per capita, industry value added, average household size and affluence, as measured by GDP per capita, are non-stationary and integrated of order (1).

Once variables of a model are classified as integrated of order I(1), and so on, it is possible to set up models that lead to stationary relations among these variables, thereby making standard inference possible. However, the necessary criterion for stationarity among non-stationary variables is called cointegration. Testing for cointegration is a necessary step to check if the modeling exercise undertaken yields empirically meaningful relationships. Thus, the next step is to conduct the cointegration tests.

Table 1. Results of unit root tests

Variables	Unit root tests	Difference order	Exogenous (α, β, k)	t-statistic	Significance level	Test critical value	Verdict
lnI	ADF	1	(α, β, 0)	-4.63	5%	-3.56	I(1)
	PP	1	(α, β, 2)	-4.64	5%	-3.56	I(1)
lnI_{va}	ADF	1	(α, 0, 0)	-6.96	5%	-2.96	I(1)
	PP	1	(α, 0, 7)	-7.63	5%	-2.96	I(1)
$lnAHHS$	ADF	1	(α, 0, 0)	-6.01	5%	-2.96	I(1)
	PP	1	(α, 0, 2)	-6.02	5%	-2.96	I(1)
lnA	ADF	1	(α, 0, 0)	-4.20	5%	-2.96	I(1)
	PP	1	(α, 0, 0)	-4.20	5%	-2.96	I(1)

Source: Authors' calculation based on the data used in the model.

Notes: ADF – Augmented Dickey Fuller; PP – Phillips-Perron.

Cointegration test

The variables CO2 emissions per capita, industry value added (as per cent of GDP), average household size and GDP per capita are all non-stationary and integrated of order (1). Hence, these variables satisfy the precondition for conducting a cointegration test and hence if there is a stable and non-spurious long-run relationship between these variables (Ramirez, 2000). Given a number of non-stationary variables of the same order, the number of cointegrated vectors, involving these variables, can be determined by the Johansen cointegration approach. The results of the Johansen maximum likelihood test of cointegration are shown in table 2. The trace test statistics of the null hypothesis of no cointegration vector against the alternative hypothesis of one cointegrating vector as provided in table 2 suggests that there is one cointegrating vector. The maximum eigenvalue test statistic also indicates the same.

The results of the unit root tests and the cointegartion tests support the existence of long-run equilibrium relationships among the variables of the model as presented in equation (4). The next step is to obtain the long-run estimates of the model. For this, the Fully Modified Ordinary Least Squares (FM-OLS) estimation procedure is used.

Table 2. Johansen cointegration test

Hypothesized number of cointegrated equation(s)	Trace statistic	0.05 per cent critical values	Maximum Eigen statistic	0.05 per cent critical values
None	55.48*	47.86	28.6*	27.58
At most 1	29.26	29.79	14.28	21.10
At most 2	14.99	15.49	11.41	14.26
At most 3	3.57	3.84	3.57	3.84

Source: Authors' calculation based on the data used in the model.

Notes: Trace test and Max-eigenvalue test indicates 1 cointegrating equation(s) at the 0.05 level.

*Denotes rejection of the hypothesis at the 0.05 level.

V. FULLY MODIFIED ORDINARY LEAST SQUARES ESTIMATION

In time series data, once the cointegration tests establish the existence of a long-run relationship among the variables, the ordinary least square (OLS) technique, if used to estimate the parameters of the model, comes up with super-consistent estimates of the parameters, for example, the estimators converge at rate equal to the sample size of the model. Furthermore, if a problem of endogeniety among the independent variables exists, then the limiting distribution of the OLS estimators is said to have the so-called second order bias terms (Phillips and Hansen, 1990). In the presence of these bias terms, inference becomes difficult. Thus, to investigate the long-run relationship among variables, various modern econometric techniques were introduced. These techniques propose modifications of OLS that result in zero mean Gaussian mixture limiting distributions that make the standard asymptotic inference feasible (Vogelsang and Wagner, 2014). One such method is the fully modified OLS (FM-OLS) approach. This method, which was introduced and developed by Phillips and Hansen (1990), uses the "Kernel" estimators of the nuisance parameters that affect the asymptotic distribution of the OLS estimator. FM-OLS modifies the least squares so as to account for the effect of serial correlation and presence of endogeniety among the independent variables (brought about by the existence of cointegration among the variables) and thereby ensures asymptotic efficiency of estimators. Thus, the FM-OLS method gives reliable estimates and provides a check for robustness of the results. Table 3 contains a report of the estimated results of the FM-OLS approach.

**Table 3. Fully modified ordinary least squared
regression results for extended STIRPAT
model as in equation (4)**

Variables	Coefficient	t test	P values
lnI_{va}	-0.39 (.359)	-1.10	0.28
$lnAHHS$	1.87* (.51)	3.67	0.00
lnA	1.14* (0.09)	12.00	0.00
Constant	-12.68* (1.21)	-5.83	0.00
Observations			32
R^2			0.967
Standard error			0.06

Source: Authors' calculation based on the data used in the model.
Notes: Dependent variable: lnI.
          Standard errors are in parenthesis.
          Significance: *$p < 0.05$, **$p < 0.01$, ***$p < 0.1$.

The FM-OLS results in table 3 reveal that the average household size and the real GDP per capita are statistically significant in explaining variations in the level of CO_2 emission per capita. In particular, both of these variables have a significantly large positive effect on the emission level. Industry value added is not statistically significant. The adjusted R^2 value is 0.967, which indicates a very good fit. The diagnostic tests reveal that the estimated residuals are I(0) and the test for serial correlation for residuals based on Q statistic reveal that there is no serial correlation present.

The FM-OLS estimates are accepted as estimators for the extended STIRPAT model (equation 4) and are used for predicting CO_2 emission in India for 2050. Based on the estimates of the model, the future total CO_2 emission is estimated to be 3,516.2 million metric tons in 2050. The estimate obtained is also in line with what is suggested by IPCC research on CO_2 levels. The IPCC reports suggest that both population and level of affluence can be significant factors in greenhouse gas emission trends in poorer countries. That is highly applicable for India as well. The present model also finds that affluence (measured as real GDP per capita) is an important variable influencing per capita carbon emission levels in India. Additionally, average household size is also found to be an important variable, resulting in higher per capita emissions in the country. Thus, based on the ongoing economic development momentum in India and a population projected to reach 1.862 billion by 2050, carbon emission levels are expected to rise sharply in the country.

As indicated by the coefficients corresponding to the independent variables, which are statistically significant in table 3, the factors affecting carbon emission per capita in India may be ranked (in terms of higher to lower in importance) as follows:

- Average household size – contribution ratio of 1.87 implying that a 1 per cent increase in average household size is likely to increase carbon emission per capita by 1.9 per cent;[9]

- Per capita GDP – contribution ratio of 1.14 implying that a 1 per cent increase in per capita GDP is likely to raise carbon emission per capita by 1.1 per cent.

The figures above present the contribution of each of the two identified drivers of per capita carbon emission in India for the entire period 1980-2012. However, it would be interesting to understand if these contributions have remained the same over the entire three decades or if they have changed over time. To do this, the same proposed model as in equation (4) is run separately for three different time periods: the first one for period 1980-1990, the second one covering the period 1990-2000 and the third one for the period 2000-2012. The results of these three models are reported in table 4.

Table 4. Fully modified ordinary least squared regression results of extended STIRPAT model as in equation (4) for three time periods, 1980-1990, 1990-2000 and 2000-2012

Period	Change in carbon emission per capita		lnI_{va}	$lnAHHS$	lnA
	Per cent	Million metric tons			
1980-1990	57.9	0.261	2.46 (1.39)	2.12 (1.85)	0.84** (0.33)
1990-2000	37.7	0.268	1.14 (0.67)	1.51 (3.31)	0.896* (0.13)
2000-2012	63.1	0.618	-0.34 (0.19)	0.57*** (0.28)	0.89* (0.06)

Source: Authors' calculation based on the data used in the model.

Notes: Dependent variable: lnI.

Standard errors are in parenthesis.

Significance: *p < 0.05, **p < 0.01, ***p < 0.1.

AHHS, average household size.

---

[9]   Given natural log transformation of both per capita carbon emission and average household size, the coefficient of 1.87 against natural log of average household size is interpreted as a 1 per cent increase in average household size multiples per capita carbon emission by $e^{1.87*ln(1.01)} = 1.0188$, i.e. a 1 per cent increase in average household size increases per capita carbon emission by a 1.9 per cent. The coefficients corresponding to other independent variables are interpreted similarly.

Table 4 shows the changes in per capita carbon emission levels over three decades from 1980 to 2012 and the respective roles of share of industry value added in GDP, average household size and per capita GDP in driving that change. Carbon emission per capita increased by 0.261 million metric tons from 1980 to 1990. This figure increased to 0.268 during the period 1990-2000. Thereafter, from 2000 to 2012, it still increased and more than doubled to stand at 0.618 million metric tons. Increasing per capita GDP has been the most important driver throughout and its influence has remained more or less constant over time. Influence of average household size became important only in the recent years. Industry value added turns out to be statistically insignificant in explaining variations in emission levels over these shorter time periods, as well. Thus, increase in GDP per capita explains the increase in the emission per capita not only for the entire period from 1980-2012 but also during the three shorter periods in between. Though the elasticity of per capita carbon emission with respect to average household size is highest for the longer period from 1980 to 2012, during the shorter periods considered, it is only in the last one and a half decade that much of the increase in the emission level has been due to an increase in the average household size. Thus, real per capita GDP has always been one of major drivers of per capita carbon emission in India.

VI. DISCUSSION

Based on the results in table 3, the rising per capita GDP and the average household size were the most important drivers of carbon emission in India over the last three decades. In particular, the influence of per average household size was the most important driver and even more influential in the recent one and a half decade.

Household size

Family and households hold a prominent place in the social life of any population as the most potent socioeconomic institution. Any change in the household size has a serious social, economic and demographic implication. The national census 2011 drew attention to falling household size during the last three decades, which is becoming an all India phenomenon, while the number of households increased at a phenomenal rate. The rate of growth of the households was close to 30 per cent during the 2001-2011 decade (Nayak and Behera, 2014). The carbon emission elasticity with respect to average household size in India is given to be 1.4 (table 3) for the entire period 1980-2012, indicating that an increase in household size is likely to have caused increased emission levels. This result varies from most of the results obtained by other researchers (Cole and Neumayer, 2004; Liddle, 2004). Though the national census 2011 drew attention to falling household sizes during the last three decades, the rural households still continue to be relatively large. Sixty-eight per cent of the population of India lives in rural areas (in 2013, according to World Development Indicators). Thus, given the results of the model, the rising household size in rural India may have been one of the major reasons for increased carbon emissions in the country. A comparison of census data of 2011 to 2001 indicates that there has been a major change in the energy consumption pattern of rural households. To meet their fuel requirement for cooking, these households have embraced the substitution of traditional fuel type (firewood, cow dung, leaves and twigs, branches, straw and rice husk) by more fossil fuel-based cooking fuel. The number of rural households using electricity also has risen substantially in recent years (55.3 per cent of the rural households used electricity as their primary energy source for lighting in 2011 as against a 43.6 per cent of the rural households in 2001 (TERI, 2013). This, together with large household sizes in these rural areas, have significantly contributed to energy demand and consequently to the levels of carbon emissions in the country.

Urban households undoubtedly may have larger energy demand as compared to rural households. Be it for cooking, water supply, sewerage network, transportation, information and communication technology or the provision of social infrastructure to enhance quality of life, energy in the form of electricity, oil and gas is an inescapable necessity for the urban population. Yet, there are some positive results pertaining to energy used by the urban population. First, over the years, urban families have moved towards more fuel efficient sources for residential use. In addition, a significant part of the educated urban middle and upper class practice energy conservation as it is a learned habit and to save money (Jain and others, 2014). Second, as the present study points out, it is the larger household size that results in larger emissions. The fact that urban household sizes have fallen over the years is thus a welcome change.

Gross domestic product per capita

The relationship between economic development and environmental pressure resembles an inverted U-shaped curve. India belongs to the middle-development range and, as such, there are likely to be strong pressures on the natural environment, mostly in the form of intensified resource consumption and the production of waste. Furthermore, higher levels of income tend to correlate with disproportionate consumption of energy and generation of greenhouse gas emission (Hunter, 2000). An increase in income and affluence in the country, as measured by GDP per capita over the years coupled with the increased population and the changing population structure, has directly affected the national level CO_2 emission through increased consumption and production activities. There is an obvious increase in consumption demand among the affluent Indians who, in turn, engage in production activities to satisfy their consumption needs. Ghosh (2010) supports the result that higher economic growth, which leads to more affluent members of the population, stimulates energy demand in end-users sectors, namely industry, transport, commerce, households and agriculture. The majority of commercial energy in India comes from coal, which generates the highest carbon dioxide emission in the country.

Share of industry value added

CO2 emissions from manufacturing industries and construction contain the emissions from the combustion of fuels in industry. Industry valued added in GDP in India rose on average from 1980 to 2012, though the country did shows signs of deindustrialization during the period 2000-2009. The share of industry, particularly manufacturing in CO2 emissions averaged about 26 per cent annually. While it ranged from 29 per cent to 34 per cent in the 1980s, more recently during the period 2000-2012, it stayed in a range of 19 to 25 per cent. However, as the model results indicate, the variations in value added of industry in GDP contributed to variations in per capita carbon emissions in the country.

VII. CONCLUSION AND POLICY DIRECTIONS

The present paper attempts to study the impact of population on carbon dioxide emission levels in India and to project the extent of emission in the country in 2050. Using an extended STIRPAT model with FM-OLS estimation techniques on data obtained from World Development Indicators and the Ministry of Statistics and Programme Implementation of the Government of India from 1980 to 2012, the CO2 emission in India for 2050 is estimated to be 3,516.2 million metric tons. It is found that the average household size and per capita GDP are important factors in determining the level of per capita carbon emission levels in the country. The elasticity of per capita carbon emissions to changes in real GDP per capita was 1.14 for the entire thirty two-year period from 1980 to 2012. When reviewed by decade, it was about 0.84 in 1990s and increased to 0.89 thereafter. Average household size caused emission levels to rise only in the last decade, but the elasticity of per capita carbon emission with respect to average household size for the entire period was much higher at 1.87. Industry value added and variations in it over this period did not appear to have had an impact on emission levels.

Gross domestic product per capita at purchasing power parity (PPP) in India averaged $3,074.12 from 1990 until 2013, reaching an all-time high of $5,238.02 in 2013 and a record low of $1,176.44 in 1991. The GDP per capita, in India (PPP) is equivalent to 29 per cent of the world's average (World Development Indicators). The GDP per capita has been growing at the rate of 5.6 per cent annually. Thus, as the growing affluence in the country in general is leading to an increased level of consumption and production activities, it is important to ensure energy conservation and emission reductions in fields of production. At the same time, the likely impact of increasing affluence, urbanization, and movement towards nuclear family system on increased per capita use of residential energy cannot be ignored. Policies need to be designed to prevent waste and encourage conservation. The policies should be structured to balance emission control and improved standards of living.

Though rural households remain relatively large in size, the median household size in urban India has been falling for some time and is now less than four for the first time in history (India, Ministry of Home Affairs, 2011). This trend coupled with the growing rate of urbanization in the country is undoubtedly good news as far as carbon emission levels are concerned. However, the larger size of rural households along with the shift in their energy consumption pattern in favour of fossil fuel based energy continues to be one of the major challenges in controlling carbon emissions in India. While a change in the consumption pattern away from traditional types is positive, the larger size of households is an unfavourable feature that unfortunately is not likely to change in the short run. Therefore, it is absolutely necessary to ensure that these rural households get increased disposable income through additional income-generating opportunities, so that they can afford more modern and efficient fuel types. At the same time, the availability and accessibility of clean fuel types in rural areas need to be ensured. The Government of India has already taken an initiative in this direction by seeking to increase the distributorship of liquefied petroleum gas (LPG) in the rural areas, but it needs to work on the affordability of rural households for using these alternate fuel types. Lastly, efforts must be made to educate rural households on the advantages of energy conservation.

With a current population growth rate of 1.58 per cent, the most serious impact on carbon emission levels in India, is undoubtedly its population size. The population grew from 868 million in 1990 (2 per cent per annum) to 1.04 billion in 2000 (1.7 per cent per annum) and further increased to 1.2 billion in 2010 (1.2 per cent per annum). The population of India represents 18 per cent of the world's total population, which arguably means that one in every six people on the planet is a resident of India. With the population growth rate at 1.58 per cent, India is predicted to have more than 1.5 billion people by the end of 2030. Every year, India adds more people than any other country in the world, and, in fact, the individual population of some of its states is equal to the total population of many countries. Some of the reasons for the country's rapidly growing population are poverty, illiteracy, the high fertility rate, a rapid decline in death rates or mortality rates and immigration from Bangladesh and Nepal.

Thus, while the growing population is obviously expected to raise the country's carbon emission levels to alarming levels, the important result that the present study comes up with is that along with the growing population, the increasing GDP per capita and changing household size magnifies the problem even more.

India, therefore, faces the enormous challenge of curbing greenhouse gases (CO2 emissions: 2.6 billion tons in 2013) as its population and economy expands and its population structure undergoes change. In 2010, India voluntarily committed to a 20 per cent to 25 per cent cut in carbon emissions relative to economic output by 2020 against 2005 levels. Under current policies, its carbon dioxide emissions will double by 2030, according to the International Energy Agency. Thus, policies that would help to reduce emissions are undoubtedly curbing population growth, but most importantly, large households in rural areas leading to greater emission levels needs to be addressed urgently. Policies towards reduced and efficient use and waste reduction with respect to both residential and commercial use of energy will definitely help in the short run.

REFERENCES

Barido, Diego Ponce de Leon, and Julian D. Marshall (2014). Relationship between urbanization and CO_2 emissions depends on income level and policy. *Environmental Science & Technology*, vol. 48, No. 7, pp. 3632-3639.

Bekhet, Hussain Ali, and Tahira Yasmin (2014). Application of urban transition theory in Malaysia economy: ARDL model approach. National Symposium & Exhibition on Business & Accounting, 19 March. Available from www.researchgate.net/publication/ 260960254_Application_of_Urban_Transition_Theory_in_Malaysia_Economy_ARDL_Model_ Approach. Accessed 12 November 2016.

Birdsall, Nancy (1992). *Another Look at Population and Global Warming*, vol. 1020 Washington, D.C.: World Bank.

Bongaarts, John (1992). Population growth and global warming. *Population and Development Review*, vol. 18, No. 2, pp. 299-319.

BP Energy Outlook (2015). BP energy outlook 2035: focus on North America, March. Available from bp.com/energy outlook #BPstats. Accessed 13 November 2015.

Cole, Matthew A., and Eric Neumayer (2004). Examining the impact of demographic factors on air pollution. *Population and Environment*, vol. 26, No. 1, pp. 5-21.

Dalton, Michael, and others (2007). Demographic change and future carbon emissions in China and India. Paper presented at the Population Association of America Annual Meetings. New York, 16 March. Available from http://paa2007.princeton.edu/papers/72123. Accessed 13 November 2015.

_____(2008). Population aging and future carbon emissions in the United States. *Energy Economics*, vol. 30, No. 2, pp. 642-675.

Dietz, Thomas, and Eugene A. Rosa (1997). Effects of population and affluence on CO_2 emissions. *Proceedings of the National Academy of Sciences of the United States of America*, vol. 94, No. 1, pp. 175-179.

Ehrlich, Paul R., and John P. Holdren (1971). Impact of population growth. *Science,* New Series, vol. 171, No. 3977, pp. 1212-1217.

The Energy and Resources Institute (TERI) (2013). TERI Energy & Environment Data Directory and Yearbook 2013/14. Available from http://bookstore.teri.res.in/docs/books/TEDDY14/ domestic/domestic.pdf. Accessed 13 November 2016.

Energy Information Agency (EIA) (2015). International Energy Statistics. Available from www.eia.gov/ beta/international/data/browser/#/?vs=INTL.44-1-AFRC-QBTU.A&vo=0&v=H&start=1980 &end=2014. Accessed 13 November 2016.

Engelman, Robert (2010). *Population, Climate Change and Women's Lives*. Worldwatch Report 183. Worldwatch Institute. Available from www.worldwatch.org/system/files/ 183%20Population%20and%20climate.pdf. Accessed 13 November 2016.

Fan, Ying, and others (2006). Analyzing impact factors of CO_2 emissions using the STIRPAT model. *Environmental Impact Assessment Review*, vol. 26, No. 4, pp. 377-395.

Gambhir, Ajay, and Gabrial Anandarajah (2013). India's CO_2 emissions pathway to 2050. Available from www.imperial.ac.uk/media/imperial-college/grantham-institute/public/publications/ institute-reports-and-analytical-notes/India's-emissions-pathways-to-2050---summary- report.pdf. Accessed 13 November 2016.

Ghosh, Sajai (2010). Examining carbon emissions economic growth nexus for India: a multivariate cointegration approach. *Energy Policy*, vol. 38, No. 6, pp. 3008-3014.

Gupta, S. (1997). *Energy Consumption and GHG Emissions: A Case Study for India.* Global Warming, Asian Energy Studies. New Delhi: The Energy and Resources Institute.

Hunter, Lori M. (2000). *The Environmental Implications of Population Dynamics.* Santa Monica, California: RAND.

India, Ministry of Home Affairs (2011). Census of India, 2011. Office of the Registrar General and Census Commissioner India. Available from http://censusindia.gov.in/. Accessed 13 November 2015.

India, Ministry of Statistics and Programme Implementation (2015a). Annual survey of industries (various issues). Available from https://india.gov.in/. Accessed 13 November 2015.

_____ (2015b). Selected socio economic statistics India, 2011. Available from https://india.gov.in/. Accessed 15 May 2015.

Intergovernmental Panel on Climate Change (IPCC) (2000). IPCC special report, emissions scenarios: summary for policymakers. Available from www.ipcc.ch/pdf/special-reports/spm/sres-en.pdf. Accessed 13 November 2016.

International Energy Agency (IEA) (2007). *International Energy Agency World Energy Outlook 2007: China and India Insights.* Paris: IEA and OECD.

Jain, Mohit, and others (2014). Energy usage attitudes of urban India. Paper presented at the 2nd Conference. Stockholm, 24-27 August. Available from www.dgp.toronto.edu/~mjain/ICT4S-2014.pdf.

Jiang, Leiwen, and Karen Hardee (2011). How do recent population trends matter to climate change? *Population Research and Policy Review*, vol. 30, No. 2, pp. 287-312.

Knapp, Tom, and Rajen Mookerjee (1996). Population growth and global CO2 emissions: a secular perspective. *Energy Policy,* vol. 24, No. 1, pp. 31-37.

Liddle, Brantley (2004). Demographic dynamics and per capita environmental impact: using panel regressions and household decompositions to examine population and transport. *Population and Environment*, vol. 26, No. 1, pp. 23-39.

_____ (2011). Consumption-driven environmental impact and age structure change in OECD countries: a cointegration-STIRPAT analysis. *Demographic Research*, vol. 24, No. 30, pp. 749-770.

_____ (2014). Impact of population, age structure, and urbanization on carbon emissions/energy consumption: evidence from macro-level, cross-country analyses. *Population and Environment*, vol. 35, No. 3, pp. 286-304.

Liddle, Brantley, and Sidney Lung (2010). Age-structure, urbanization, and climate change in developed countries: revisiting STIRPAT for disaggregated population and consumption-related environmental impacts. *Population and Environment*, vol. 31, No. 5, pp. 317-343.

MacKellar, F. Landis, and others (1995). Population, households and CO2 emissions. *Population and Development Review*, vol. 21, No. 4, pp. 849-865.

Martínez-Zarzoso, Inmaculada, and Antonello Maruotti (2011). The impact of urbanization on CO2 emissions: evidence from developing countries. *Ecological Economics*, vol. 70, No. 7, pp. 1344-1353.

Mukhopadhyay, Kakali (2001). An empirical analysis of the sources of CO2 emission changes in India during 1973-74 to 1996-97. *Asian Journal of Energy and Environment*, vol. 2, No. 3-4, pp. 231-269.

_____ (2002). A structural decomposition analysis of air pollution from fossil fuel combustion in India. *International Journal of Environment and Pollution*, vol. 18, No. 5, pp. 486-497.

_____ (2011). Air pollution and household income distribution in India: pre- and post-reform (1983-1984 to 2006-2007). *Journal of Energy and Development,* vol. 35, No. 1/2, pp. 315-339.

Mukhopadhyay, Kakali, and Debech Chakraborty (2002). Economic reforms, energy consumption changes and CO2 emission in India: a quantitative analysis. *Asia-Pacific Development Journal*, vol. 9, No. 2, pp. 107-129.

_____ (2004). Energy consumption changes and CO2 emission in India during reforms. *Journal of Quantitative Economics*, vol. 2, No. 1, pp. 55-87.

Murthy, N. Satyanarayana, Manoj M. Panda, and Kirit Parikh (1997). Economic growth, energy demand and CO2 emissions in India: 1990-2020. *Environment and Development Economics*, vol. 2, No. 2, pp. 173-193.

Nayak, Debendra K., and Rabi B. Behera (2014). Changing household size in India: an inter-State comparison. *Transactions of the Institute of Indian Geographers*, vol. 36, No. 1, pp. 1-18.

Ozturk, Ilhan, and Gazi Salah Uddin (2012). Causality among carbon emissions, energy consumption and growth in India. *Ekonomska Istraživanja*, vol. 25, No. 3, pp. 752-775.

Phillips, Peter C.B., and Bruce Hansen (1990). Statistical inference in instrumental variables regression with I(1) processes. *The Review of Economic Studies*, vol. 57, No. 1, pp. 99-125.

Poumanyvong, Phetkeo, and Shinji Kaneko (2010). Does urbanization lead to less energy use and lower CO2 emissions? A cross-country analysis. *Ecological Economics*, vol. 70, No. 2, pp. 434-444.

Ramirez, Miguel D. (2000). Foreign direct investment in Mexico: a cointegration analysis. *Journal of Development Studies*, vol. 37, No. 1, pp. 138-162.

Raskin, Paul D. (1995). Methods for estimating the population contribution to environmental change. *Ecological Economics,* vol. 15, No. 3, pp. 225-233.

Roberts, Tyler D. (2014). Intergenerational transfers in US county-level CO2 emissions, 2007. *Population and Environment*, vol. 35, No. 4, pp. 365-390.

Satterthwaite, David (2009). The implications of population growth and urbanization for climate change. *Environment and Urbanization,* vol. 21, No. 2, pp. 545-567.

Shi, Anqing (2003). The impact of population pressure on global carbon dioxide emissions, 1975-1996: evidence from pooled cross-country data. *Ecological Economics*, vol. 44, No. 1, pp. 29-42.

Shukla, P.R. (2006). India's GHG emission scenarios: aligning development and stabilization paths. *Current Science-Bangalore*, vol. 90, No. 3, pp. 384-395.

United Nations (1993). *Report of the United Nations Conference on Environment and Development, Rio de Janeiro, 3-14 June 1992*, vol. I, *Resolutions Adopted by the Conference.* United Nations publication, Sales No. E.93.I.8, and corrigendum, resolution 1, annex II.

Vogelsang, Timothy J., and Martin Wagner (2014). Integrated modified OLS estimation and fixed-b inference for cointegrating regressions. *Journal of Econometrics*, vol. 178, No. 2, pp. 741-760.

Wei, Taoyuan (2011). What STIRPAT tells about effects of population and affluence on the environment? *Ecological Economics*, vol. 72, No. 2011, pp. 70-74.

World Bank (2015). A comparative analysis: challenges and opportunities for large higher education systems. Report commissioned by the British Council in partnership with the Centre for Policy Research in Higher Education at the National University of Educational Planning and Administration in New Delhi. New Delhi, India: UNESCO. Available from www.britishcouncil.org/sites/default/files/3.6_managing-large-systems.pdf.

Yeo, Yeongjun, and others (2015). Driving forces of CO2 emissions in emerging countries: LMDI decomposition analysis on China and India's residential sector. *Sustainability*, vol. 7, No. 12, pp. 16108-16129.

York, Richard, Eugene A. Rosa, and Thomas Dietz (2002). Bridging environmental science with environmental policy: plasticity of population, affluence, and technology. *Social Science Quarterly*, vol. 83, No. 1, pp. 18-34.

_____ (2003a). Bridging environmental science with environmental policy: plasticity of population, affluence, and technology. *Social Science Quarterly*, vol. 83, No. 1, pp. 18-34.

_____ (2003b). STIRPAT, IPAT and ImPACT: analytic tools for unpacking the driving forces of environmental impacts. *Ecological Economics*, vol. 46, No. 3, pp. 351-365.

Zhu, Qin, and Xizhe Peng (2012). The impacts of population change on carbon emissions in China during 1978-2008. *Environmental Impact Assessment Review*, vol. 36, pp. 1-8.

Asia-Pacific Development Journal							Vol. 23, No. 1, June 2016

THE ADMINISTRATIVE EFFICIENCY OF CONDITIONAL CASH TRANSFER PROGRAMMES: EVIDENCE FROM THE *PANTAWID PAMILYANG PILIPINO PROGRAM*

*Ma. Cecilia L. Catubig, Renato A. Villano and Brian Dollery**

The present paper examines the administrative efficiency of implementing the Pantawid Pamilyang Pilipino Program (4Ps) in the Philippines. Using data collected at a municipal level for four provinces in the Davao Region, administrative efficiency scores were computed, employing cost transfer ratios (CTR) and data envelopment analysis (DEA) for the individual municipal operations offices (MOOs) implementing the programme. CTR estimates showed that the greatest proportion of total expenditure in cash transfer programmes was direct cash transfers, which implied an efficient use of programme funding. The DEA results showed an average technical efficiency score of 0.905, which implied that there was significant potential to further improve the performance of delivery of 4Ps. The results revealed that relatively high technical efficiency scores of MOOs did not necessarily translate into a more cost-efficient implementation of the programme. Nevertheless, a positive correlation was found between CTR and the high technical efficiency scores of the MOOs implementing the programme.

JEL classification: C14, I31, I38.

Keywords: Pantawid Pamilyang Pilipino Program (4Ps), Philippines, data envelopment analysis (DEA), cost transfer ratios, cash transfers.

---

* Ma. Cecilia L. Catubig, is corresponding author and a PhD student at the UNE Business School, University of New England, Armidale, NSW 2351 Australia and an associate professor of economics at the Davao Oriental State College of Science and Technology, Davao, Philippines (e-mail: mcatubig@myune.edu.au and mcatubig15@gmail.com); Renato A. Villano is an associate professor of economics at the UNE Business School, University of New England, Armidale, NSW 2351, Australia (e-mail: rvillan2@une.edu.au); Brian Dollery is a professor of economics at the University of New England, Armidale, NSW 2351, Australia and also a member the Faculty of Economics at the Yokohama National University, Japan (e-mail: bdollery@une.edu.au). The present paper has benefited from constructive comments provided by three anonymous referees associated with this Journal.

I. INTRODUCTION

The use of social cash transfers to assist extremely poor and vulnerable people has become widespread in developing countries, including the Philippines. However, these programmes are often criticized as being expensive and inefficient and for encouraging welfare dependency. For instance, Grosh (1994) and Coady, Perez and Vera-llamas (2005) stress that administrative costs consume a high proportion of the overall cost of these programmes, mainly because of the complexity involved in administering cash transfers, especially the targeting of transfers and monitoring beneficiaries. By contrast, advocates of these programmes emphasize their success in practice. For example, Kakwani, Veras Soares and Son (2005) argue that not only have conditional cash transfer (CCT) programmes increased the incomes of poor people in the short run and improved the capabilities of recipients in both the medium and long run, they have also proved to be cost-effective.

O'Brien (2014) argues that the cost of CCT programmes is important as cost-effectiveness matters. Maximizing the impact of scarce funds on CCT objectives is essential. However, minimizing costs is only one factor. Most evaluation studies of CCTs have focused on the effectiveness and the efficiency of the programmes, concepts that are related to the cost of delivering programmes. In principle, the cost of programme delivery includes the cash transfer itself, the salaries and wages of staff, travelling expenses and other administrative costs. These costs vary depending on the country adopting CCTs and on the extent of programme delivery.

In the case of the Philippines, the *Pantawid Pamilyang Pilipino Program* (4Ps) budget in 2014 reached 62.6 billion Philippine pesos (Pts) ($1.29 billion), making it the third largest (about four million households) CCT programme globally after the one in Brazil (8.8 million households) and the one in Mexico (6.5 million households) (Albert, 2014). The continued increase in the budget allocation for this poverty alleviation programme of the Department of Social Welfare and Development (DSWD) has been under scrutiny since its implementation in 2008. This is hardly surprising as the administrative efficiency and effectiveness of public expenditure is a matter of legitimate public concern. Evaluating the efficiency of expenditure requires an assessment of the relationship between inputs and outputs and the cost of delivery of CCT programmes, including operational and administrative costs. In particular, administration costs are a useful indicator of productive (in)efficiency. Assessing efficiency can serve as a first step towards strengthening CCT performance. Given that 4Ps is in its seventh year, it is timely to evaluate the administrative efficiency of the agency implementing the programme, which is the main objective of the present paper. An evaluation exercise of this kind can assist public policymakers by generating a better understanding of the cost of implementing 4Ps and offering recommendations for improving the efficient use of resources, especially to determine the extension of support to children in high school up to 18 years old and for enhancing the operation of the programme in the future.

Despite earlier work undertaken by Fiszbien and others (2009) and Devereux and Pelham (2005), no agreed approach to assessing cost efficiency exists. Nonetheless, Handa and Davis (2006) have called for more cost-efficiency studies of cash transfer programmes, including comparisons with other types of programmes. The existing empirical literature on CCT cost-efficiency analysis hinges on the methodology advanced by Caldes, Coady and Maluccio (2006), who evaluated the cost efficiency of three similar poverty alleviation programmes in Latin America by considering the cost of making a one-unit transfer to a beneficiary, referred to as cost transfer ratio (CTR). In the present study, cost efficiency and CTR as a composite indicator of administrative efficiency are used.

This paper seeks to contribute to the empirical literature in two main ways. First, following Caldes, Coady and Maluccio (2006), estimates of cost transfer ratios are obtained for each set (Set 1 to Set 6) of programme implementation as a baseline on programmatic efficiency. Second, a non-parametric approach is employed to examine the cost efficiency of the municipal operations offices (MOOs) implementing the programme. These two measures are used to examine the administrative efficiency of the office. Specifically, the paper intends to (a) evaluate the components of the total spending per beneficiary and decompose this based on administration costs direct cash transfer, capacity development, and monitoring and evaluation cost by estimating cost transfer ratios, (b) examine the average annual implementation cost per beneficiary, (c) obtain technical and cost-efficiency scores of MOOs implementing the programme and (d) compare the actual implementation costs of 4Ps with the costs from similar programmes in other countries.

The paper is divided into four main parts. Section II contains a synoptic review of the conceptual, empirical and institutional perspectives on cash transfer programmes and the methodologies used in cost-efficiency analysis. In section III, the methods of analysis are discussed while in section IV, the empirical results and findings of the study are presented. The paper ends in section V with some brief conclusions.

II. CONCEPTUAL, EMPIRICAL AND INSTITUTIONAL PERSPECTIVES ON CASH TRANSFER PROGRAMMES

Brief overview of the *Pantawid Pamilyang Pilipino Program*

The *Pantawid Pamilyang Pilipino Program* is closely patterned on successful CCTs in Latin American programmes, sharing the objectives of social assistance and social development, both of which are central to the poverty reduction and social protection strategy of the Government of the Philippines. To help build human capital, the prime focus of the programme, short-term income support is extended to extremely poor eligible households contingent on their compliance with the programme's conditions, such as enrolment in school (children 6-14 years old) and regular visits to health centres (pregnant women and children 0-5 years old). A household can be a recipient of 4Ps provided the following criteria are met: (a) it is a resident in programme areas of 4Ps; (b) it is identified as poor based on proxy means test (PMT); and (c) at least one member of the household is below 15 years old at the time of the enrolment into the programme or a pregnant woman.

The *Pantawid Pamilyang Pilipino Program* began as a pilot programme of the Department of Social Welfare and Development (DSWD) in 2007 (Fernandez and Olfindo, 2011). It was launched as a full-scale cash transfer programme in February 2008, covering 330,000 beneficiaries in Set 1 and then scaled up in 2009 to cover another 320,000 households in Set 2. In less than three years, the programme's household beneficiaries grew to about 1.9 million (Velarde and Fernandez, 2011) and by 2014, it had covered around four million households.

Design features of the *Pantawid Pamilyang Pilipino Program*

The design features of 4Ps include targeting methods and monitoring conditionalities, which are similar to the design characteristics employed in other countries that have adopted CCTs. The 4Ps targeting system is centrally managed by DSWD through the National Household Targeting Systems for Poverty Reduction (NHTS-PR). It follows a multi-step process in the selection of beneficiaries wherein the poorest provinces are selected first, based on official poverty incidence taken from a survey conducted by the National Statistics Office (Fernandez and Olfindo, 2011). The poorest municipalities from the poorest provinces are identified based on the poverty incidence of small area estimates (SAE). From the poorest municipalities, total household enumeration or a household targeting system is used to identify poor households within the selected *barangay*.[1] The poorest household is finally selected

---

[1] *Barangay* is the smallest administrative division in the Philippines. It is a native Filipino term for a village, district or ward.

using a proxy means testing that assesses household socioeconomic characteristics. Household names are then published at a *barangay* hall for community validation before they are finally enrolled in the programme. From this step onward, the implementation of 4Ps is decentralized and it is the various regions and provinces that are responsible for the final enrolment of qualified beneficiaries, release cash transfers and monitor their compliance to conditionalities.

According to Fernandez and Olfindo (2011), the numerous conditions imposed by 4Ps make this CCT unique among other CCT models. In addition to enrolment and school attendance of children aged 6 to 14 years old plus regular check-ups for children aged 0 to 5 years old and pregnant women, DSWD has added the conditions of pre-school or day care centre attendance for children aged 3 to 5 years old, taking of de-worming pills for 6- to 14-year-old children and parental attendance at family development sessions. Whereas these conditions are meant to enhance the programme's impact, they also inevitably add to administrative costs and the burden of monitoring participants' compliance.

Empirical approaches to cash transfer programmes

While considerable literature has evaluated the impact of cash transfer programmes, there is little empirical evidence on their cost structures and limited assessment of the cost efficiency and cost effectiveness of cash transfer programmes. Comparability between empirical studies cannot be carried out because the work undertaken on cost structure evaluation is scant. Even on the same kind of programmes, wide variations in what costs are included in the calculations abound, with some limited to administrative costs only, while other studies have focused on losses and leakages associated with particular programme. There are also variations in the cost of delivering the cash transfer programme in terms of the proportion of total spending absorbed by administration and implementation costs. Table 1 contains a summary of the various cost-efficiency studies on cash transfer programmes.

These cost-efficiency studies determined CTR of the cash transfer programme and the cost expended for every unit of cash transferred to household beneficiaries. The results were varied. A plausible reason for this cost variation could be that each CCT programme is different in design and implementation. Moreover, the reported cost for different studies may not include the costs of planning and evaluation.

In addition, most studies emphasize the difficulties in obtaining reliable information on cost effectiveness. This can be attributed to the fact that cost effectiveness of social protection programmes is hard to determine, partly because full costs are difficult to obtain and partly because effectiveness is difficult to attribute

Table 1. Cost-efficiency studies

Cost-efficiency studies	CCT programmes	Cost structures in programme implementation	Cost transfer ratios (average, in US$)
Caldes and Maluccio (2005)	Red de Proteccion Social (RPS), Nicaragua (pilot)	**Programme administration costs** – consultant and staff salaries, operating costs, equipment, training and technical assistance, incorporation assemblies, targeting, external evaluation, food security transfer delivery fees, education transfer delivery fees and financial costs **Programme transfers** – total demand side transfers and total supply side transfers	RPS – 0.629
Caldes, Coady and Maluccio (2006)	RPS, Nicaragua; PROGRESA, Mexico and PRAF II, Honduras	**Programme administration costs** – programme design and planning, identification of beneficiaries, incorporation of beneficiaries, delivery of demand transfers, delivery of supply transfers, conditionality, monitoring and evaluation and external evaluation **Programme transfers** – demand side transfers and supply side transfers	RPS – 0.629 PROGRESA – 0.106 PRAF II – 0.499
Ellis, Devereux and White (2009)	Malawi Dowa Emergency Cash Transfers; Zambia Social Cash Transfers	**Administration costs** – management, targeting, registration, delivery of transfers, monitoring and evaluation and conditionality **Programme transfers** – demand side transfers and supply side transfers	Malawi – 1.52 Zambia (Kazungula) – 1.30 Zambia (Chipata) – 1.11
Coady, Perez and Vera-llamas (2005)	PROGRESA	**Programme administration costs** – programme design and planning, identification of beneficiaries, incorporation of beneficiaries, delivery of demand transfers, delivery of supply	PROGRESA – 0.111

Table 1. *(continued)*

Cost-efficiency studies	CCT programmes	Cost structures in programme implementation	Cost transfer ratios (average, in US$)
		transfers, conditionality, monitoring and evaluation and external evaluation	
		Programme transfers – demand side transfers and supply side transfers	

Sources: Caldes and Maluccio (2005); Caldes, Coady and Maluccio (2006); Ellis, Devereux and White (2009); and Coady, Perez and Vera-llamas (2005).

and quantify (Devereux and Pelham, 2005; Davies, 2009; Caldes, Coady and Maluccio, 2006). Hence, most of these studies focused on cost efficiency rather than cost effectiveness.

The method used in cost-efficiency analysis of CCT programmes is the cost transfer ratio (CTR), which is the ratio of non-transfer programme costs to total programme transfers. Most Latin American CCT programmes have been evaluated using this mode of analysis developed by Caldes, Coady and Maluccio (2006). The focus of the analysis is on the level and structure of costs, which are mainly based on existing accounting data. However, this empirical literature contains various evaluations emphasizing the details of the programme cost structures. The relationship between programme costs and activities needs further consideration to ensure a correct evaluation.

The methodologies in evaluating cost efficiency are limited to cash transfer programmes, but there are a number of cost-efficiency studies in the broader empirical literature dealing with the banking sector, the health sector, electricity distribution and local government (Karimzadeh, 2012; Giokas, 2002; Cheng, Bjorndal and Bjorndal, 2014; Fiorentino, Karmann and Koetter, 2006; De Borger and Kerstens, 1996; Worthington, 2000; Al-Jarrah, 2007). Most of these studies employed a non-parametric approach, commonly using the data envelopment analysis (DEA) framework. DEA measures indicators of efficiency of a given organization relative to the performance of other organizations that produce the same good or service rather than against an idealized standard of performance. The most common efficiency indicator — technical efficiency — is measured by building up the productive frontier and, if the prices of input are attainable, cost efficiency can be measured as the dual of the technical efficiency.

III. METHODS OF ANALYSIS

Analytical framework

A two-step process is used to examine the administrative efficiency. First, the indicator proposed by Caldes, Coady and Maluccio (2006) is employed whereby CTR is used. In calculating CTRs, identification of the costs and transfers to include in the estimation and how to measure them are critical. In the analysis, different programme activities were described. These activities were classified according to the nature of their costs in order to provide a picture of the cost structures of a newly implemented or mature programme. Cost analysis commenced on the implementation phase and the costs of activities prior to implementation, such as targeting of beneficiaries, are not considered. While it would have been useful to include the cost of targeting in the cost analysis, the targeting activity was done at the national level. As a result, there are no cost data at the regional level. This made it impossible to analyse the detailed cost structures from design and planning of the programme up to monitoring and evaluation (M&E). The scope of the regional programme activities commenced on the implementation of the programme, such as identification and registration of beneficiaries.

After the identification of programme activities, accounting costs were then associated with these activities, followed by the estimation of CTR, activity cost shares and activity cost transfer ratios. The costs of the different programme activities, including the total costs of direct cash transfers, were summarized over the period 2008-2013. CTR was computed as the total non-transfer programme costs divided by the total programme cash transfers, while the activity cost shares were calculated as the fraction of costs devoted to each programme activity (excluding the cash transfers). By contrast, the activity cost transfer ratio was obtained by multiplying the cost share for each activity with the aggregate CTR for all activities. The total annual cost per beneficiary was obtained by taking the ratio of the total annual programme cost and the total beneficiary per set of implementation.

Second, a DEA approach is used to obtain administrative efficiency scores of local government units (LGUs) implementing 4Ps. DEA is a non-parametric linear programming procedure whereby each decision-making unit (DMU), namely LGU in this study, is benchmarked against the best performing LGUs. The best performing LGU is identified based on the information on the specified output and the inputs used in the process. There are basically two procedures on how to implement the DEA approach to cost-efficiency analysis. First is to obtain the relative technical efficiency (TE) scores using the efficiency measures introduced by Charnes, Cooper and Rhodes (1978). Consider N municipalities each producing M different outputs using K inputs. The envelopment form of the output-oriented DEA linear programming is specified subsequently:

$$\text{Max}_{\theta,\lambda}\theta \tag{1}$$

Subject to: $\theta y_i - Y\lambda \leq 0,$

$-x_i + X\lambda \leq 0,$

$-\lambda \leq 0,$

where, y_i is the vector of outputs produced by the ith municipality, x_i is the vector of inputs used by the ith municipality, Y is the MxN ouput matrix for all N municipalities, X is a KxN input matrix for all N municipalities, i runs from 1 to N, θ is a scalar and λ is a $Nx1$ vector of constants. The value of θ is the efficiency score for a particular municipality and it should satisfy $\theta \leq 1$, with the value of 1 indicating a point on the frontier, and hence a technically efficient municipality. The DEA efficiency score for a specific DMU is not defined by an absolute standard; it is measured with respect to empirically constructed efficient frontier by the best performing DMUs. The second procedure is to calculate cost efficiency (CE) with respect to this DEA dual reference technology. As the price of input used for each LGU is known, then the cost-efficiency score for each observation can be calculated by solving N linear programmes of the form:

$$\text{Minimize} \quad \sum_{k=1}^{K} P_{Kn} X_{Kn} \tag{2}$$

$W_1 \ldots, w_n, x_{ln} \ldots, X_{kn}$

Subject to:

$$\sum_{j=1}^{N} W_j Y_{ij} - Y_{1n} \leq 0 \qquad i = 1, \ldots I$$

$$\sum_{j=1}^{N} W_j X_{kj} - X_{kn} \leq 0 \qquad k = 1, \ldots K$$

$W_j \geq 0 \; j = 1 \ldots N$

where, $P_{ln}, \ldots P_{kn}$ are the input prices (salary/wages) for the k input (labour) that unit n utilizes. This linear programme chooses the input quantities that minimize n's total costs subject to a feasibility constraint and assuming that the inputs prices it faces are fixed. The solution vector to (2) x^*_{ln}, is x^*_{kn}, n's cost-minimizing level of inputs given its input prices and output level. A score of 1 for this index would indicate that an organization is cost-efficient (SCRCSSP, 1997).

In the empirical literature on cash transfer programmes, there is no consensus regarding identification of the input and output variables to use in the cost-efficiency evaluation. In the analysis, input and output variables were identified based on the nature and the process of how the cash transfer is being implemented, such as the inputs used to achieve the necessary outputs and the purpose of the programme. In this paper, inputs are normalized in order to come up with a common basis for measurement. The following set of inputs, outputs and input prices are used to quantify the administrative efficiency of LGUs implementing 4Ps:

- Inputs: total person-days for administrative staff, total person-days for social workers/municipal links and total travel days;
- Outputs: registered beneficiaries and the amount of cash transfer disbursed;

Input prices: average daily wage of administrative staff, average daily wage of social workers/municipal links and travelling expenses per day.

Table 2 provides the basic information about the variables used in the DEA analysis, the description of variables and the selected descriptive statistics.

An average of 2,341 4Ps beneficiaries per quarter or about 780 beneficiaries per month were registered in each municipality. Considering that the total average person-days utilized by the administrative staff, social workers and municipal links

Table 2. Variables and selected descriptive statistics

Variable description	Mean	Standard deviation
Outputs		
Registered beneficiaries	2 341.33	2 356.44
Amount disbursed (in million Philippine pesos (Pts))	4.61	5.86
Inputs		
Administrative staff – total person-days	530.22	57.79
Social workers/municipal and city links – total person-days	670.14	213.41
Total travel days	64.6	29.64
Input prices		
Average daily wage – admin staff (in Pts10 000)	43.78	5.74
Average daily wage – social workers/municipal and city links (in Pts10 000)	64.43	18.35
Travelling expenses per day (in Pts10 000)	6.41	2.94

Source: Authors' own compilation.

amounts to 1,200 person-days quarterly per municipality, it can be interpreted that for every person-day, there is an average of two beneficiaries being registered. While no similar indicator can be found in the empirical literature in terms of beneficiaries registered in person-days, given the detailed data in this study, the MOO of Malita was notably different from the other MOOs as it was able to register more than two beneficiaries per person-day. This explains why it has high technical and cost-efficiency scores.

The average amount disbursed in 4Ps implementation is Pts4.61 million, or about Pts1,968 monthly per beneficiary. Each MOO worker implementing the programme utilized an average of 65 travel days in each quarter, or about 21 days in a month, spending an average of Pts21,300 each month for travelling expenses. With regard to the total expenses for the wages of the administrative staff and social workers/municipal links, a daily average wage of Pts826 and Pts961 were spent, respectively.

Data and study area

The Davao Region served as a "case study", as it could shed light for all regions and provinces with similar characteristics, namely the poorest provinces (28 provinces) and poorest municipalities (140 municipalities) based on poverty incidence above 60 per cent (Fernandez and Olfindo, 2011) implementing 4Ps, given that the structure and implementation guidelines of the cash transfer programme is the same for all areas. Davao was also suitable as a "case study" as 50 per cent of the municipalities in the four provinces of the Davao Region were covered in the first three phases of implementation. This study used a secondary, pooled cross-section administrative data collected from the four provinces of the Davao Region: Davao del Sur, Davao del Norte, Compostela Valley and Davao Oriental. The Davao Region is designated as Region XI. It is on the south-eastern portion of Mindanao and consists of five provinces[2] with Davao City as the regional capital. It is also the largest city on Mindanao. Pooled cross-section data were used as they can be useful for evaluating the impact of policy interventions and also because observations across different time periods allow for policy analysis. While there are a total of 48 municipalities in all four provinces, only 24 municipalities were included in the sample. As the implementation of 4Ps was done on a per set basis, the municipalities included in the sample are those that belong to Set 1, 2 and 3 phases. The period covered varies for each set as follows: Set 1 (2008-2014); Set 2 (2009-2014) and Set 3 (2010-2014). This is because the start of programme implementation for each set also differs. As the data obtained

---

[2]   The Davao Region consist of five provinces namely Compostela Valley; Davao del Norte; Davao del Sur; Davao Oriental; and the newly created Davao Occidental. For this study, LGUs in Davao Occidental are still part of Davao del Sur.

were on a per quarter basis, (most municipalities in the sample started at the middle of the year), there are a total of 475 observations.

The study aimed to cover at least a five-year period of implementation as this was the duration of the programme, while the succeeding sets of implementation (Sets 4 to 6) had only been implemented for less than two years. However, in estimating cost transfer ratios, the succeeding sets were included in order to show a comparison of costs of varying phases of 4Ps implementation (five years implementation versus two years implementation).

In order to analyse 4Ps cost structures, the various implementation costs data, such as administrative costs, training costs, advocacy costs and monitoring and evaluation costs, were obtained from the accounting and budget data of DSWD. Total cash transfers (direct cash transfer) data were obtained by summarizing the actual payroll of 4Ps beneficiaries for the period 2008-2013 provided by DSWD. These data were the important elements for the estimates of CTR, activity cost shares, the activity cost transfer ratio and the total annual cost per beneficiary.

IV. RESULTS AND FINDINGS ESTIMATES OF COST TRANSFER RATIOS, ACTIVITY COST SHARES, ACTIVITY COST TRANSFER RATIO AND TOTAL COST PER BENEFICIARY

Using the information on programme costs, table 3 contains CTRs of 4Ps' costs on a per set basis. The estimates of CTR show that the average CTR for 4Ps (from Set 1 to Set 6) is 0.090, which implies that, on average, only 9.0 cents were spent on the non-transfer programme cost for every peso transferred to beneficiaries. CTR can be expressed in percentage terms using the alpha ratio, namely the administrative cost as a percentage of total budget, which means that a CTR of 0.90 is about 8.2 per cent of the total budget that was absorbed by non-transfer programme costs.[3] A model averaging technique was employed to assess robustness in terms of the entire set of empirical evidence, thus even if the data of the last year were removed, the result still would yield almost the same CTR. The CTR results were presented on a per set basis while the computation of CTRs were done on an annual average based on the number of years each set was implemented. There is thus no significant difference in the value of CTRs, even if each set does not have a similar number of years of programme coverage. A summary of the computed 4Ps costs on a per set and a per year basis is presented in the annex.

---

[3]   This is calculated as 9.0/(100+9.0) = 0.082. CTR is always greater than the percentage of administrative costs for positive transfer levels (Caldes and Maluccio, 2005).

Table 3. 4Ps costs in US dollars, per set

Cost structures/set	Set 1 (2008-2013)	Set 2 (2009-2013)	Set 3 (2009-2013)	Set 4 (2011-2013)	Set 5 (2013)	Set 6 (2013)	Total
Total non-transfer programme costs	1 167 040	2 068 755	2 600 201	2 719 968	708 493	1 252 512	10 516 969
Total programme cash Transfers	10 500 137	38 353 074	9 504 922	42 218 205	11 579 857	4 272 284	116 428 479
Cost transfer ratio (CTR)	0.111	0.054	0.274	0.064	0.061	0.293	0.090
Admin cost as percentage of the total budget	9.9	5.1	21.5	6.0	5.7	22.7	8.2

Source: Authors' own compilation.

Note: 4Ps figures are translated into US dollars using an average exchange rate of Pts47.03 per $1 from 1998 to 2014.

The following programme activities (after targeting) were identified and implemented at the regional level: (a) programme delivery, which includes such activities as the identification and registration of beneficiaries, calculation of cash transfers and beneficiaries informed of the scheduled payout; (b) trainings for programme partners, DSWD workers and 4Ps beneficiaries; (c) information, education and communication (IEC)/advocacy, which covers stakeholders' visit, a volunteers congress, press conferences, production of brochures, leaflets and fan flyers, radio and TV advertisements and consultation; and (d) monitoring and evaluation. The associated costs per programme activity were summed and the activity cost shares (the fraction of costs for each activity) were calculated. The 4Ps activity cost shares are shown in table 4.

As expected, a large proportion of the cost shares were devoted to the delivery of the programme. Over the span of the three years of implementation of Sets 1 to 3, the cost share of programme delivery decreased from 92 per cent to 56 per cent. This can be attributed to a decline in some of the administrative costs, such as travelling expenses, supplies and materials, freight expenses and repairs and maintenance. However, increases in the cost share of programme delivery for the period 2011-2013 were expected following the implementation of 4Ps in LGUs covering Set 4, Set 5 and Set 6, respectively. The cost of services derived from additional social workers and municipal links for each LGU absorbs much of the cost shares. Accordingly, there is an expected increase every time 4Ps commence implementation in a local

Table 4. *Pantawid Pamilyang Pilipino Program* activity cost shares

Programme activity	2008	2009	2010	2011	2012	2013
Programme delivery (identification and registration of beneficiaries, delivery of cash transfers)	0.92	0.89	0.56	0.69	0.62	0.85
Trainings of partners, workers and beneficiaries	0.04	0.03	0.42	0.29	0.33	0.10
Advocacy/IEC	0.04	0.03	0.01	0.01	0.01	0.02
Monitoring and evaluation	–	0.05	0.01	0.01	0.04	0.03
Total	**1.00**	**1.00**	**1.00**	**1.00**	**1.00**	**1.00**

Source: Authors' own calculation.

government unit. It is interesting to note that a significant cost share for training was posted in 2010 and 2012. Detailed data show that much of the training of workers, programme partners and beneficiaries, such as capacity-building, team building, basic orientation and municipal workshops, were carried out in 2010 when the 4Ps implementation system was already in place and more workers were hired solely for 4Ps implementation. Moreover, it was observed that this training was done a year prior to a new roll out of implementation for new LGUs covered, as in the case of Set 4 in 2011 and Set 5 and Set 6 in 2013. The cost share of monitoring and evaluation was noticeably low, at an average cost of only 2.8 per cent, as it dealt with institutional strengthening expenses, such as grievance forums, cluster meetings and dialogues, while other monitoring costs for activities, such as checking conditionality, became part of the functions of social workers and assigning costs for each function/task is not possible because they cut across programme activities.

The annual activity cost transfer ratio was also computed in order to determine the costs associated with each programme activity per one unit transferred to the beneficiary. This is the cost share for each activity multiplied by the aggregate cost transfer ratios for all activities. As indicated in table 5, the patterns of the activity cost transfer ratio on a per year basis showed little difference from the cost transfer ratio on a per set basis.

Programme delivery and training activities show that, on average, only 8.7 cents and 2.3 cents, respectively, were spent for every peso of cash transferred to a beneficiary. For the two remaining programme activities, the average activity CTR is only about 1 cent per one unit cash transferred. The value of CTR of 4Ps is not noticeably different from CTRs in Latin American countries, though they are not comparable due to different implementation strategies. Hence, the results

Table 5. *Pantawid Pamilyang Pilipino Program* activity cost transfer ratio

Programme activity	2008	2009	2010	2011	2012	2013	Average
Programme delivery (identification and registration of beneficiaries)	0.20	0.05	0.06	0.07	0.05	0.09	0.087
Trainings of partners, workers and beneficiaries	0.01	0.01	0.05	0.03	0.03	0.01	0.023
Advocacy/IEC	0.01	0.01	0.01	0.01	0.01	0.01	0.010
Monitoring and evaluation		0.01	0.01	0.01	0.01	0.01	0.010
Total	0.22	0.08	0.13	0.12	0.10	0.12	0.130

Source: Authors' own calculation.

demonstrate that a greater proportion of the programme's budget is spent on the direct cash transfer itself and not much on administrative cost, as pointed out by Grosh (1994). For all the activities, the programme spent 13 cents for every dollar transferred to a household, equivalent to around 11.5 per cent of the total budget that is absorbed by the costs of different programme activities. A breakdown of cost for every US$1 transfer is shown in figure1.

Figure 1. Breakdown of cost per US$1 transfer

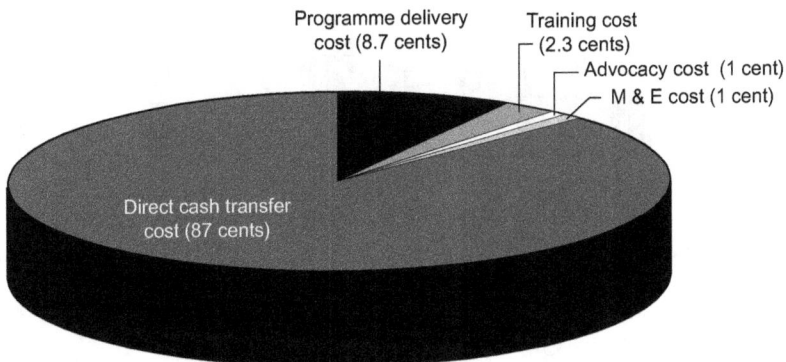

Source: Authors' own calculation.

The results of the total cost per beneficiary on a per set basis as presented in figure 2 show a declining cost trend from Set 1 to Set 6, which could in part be due to the scale effect. One reason for the decline in total cost per beneficiary is that most fixed costs are incurred during the initial phase of implementation. Thus, average fixed costs over the years of 4Ps implementation were spread out, resulting in lower cost per beneficiary. This is reflected in Son (2008, p. 4). Another reason is that during the first phase of implementation, few beneficiaries were registered, as the system and process of implementation had only been set up recently, resulting in lower efficiency. As expected, after almost five years of 4Ps implementation, during which time the management system became fully established, programme implementation for Set 6 was less costly. 4Ps implementation in the Davao Region yielded a total cost of $126.945 million (2008-2013) and reached 206,776 household-beneficiaries. The total cost per beneficiary was about $613.93, of which $50.86 comprised non-cash transfer costs and the rest, $563.07, comprised direct cash transfer (the alpha-ratio is 91.7 per cent). The average annual total cost/beneficiary is $265.88 (approximately Pts12,504.10 annually or Pts1,042.01 monthly), which is expected as the maximum monthly allocation per beneficiary is about Pts1,400.00.

Figure 2. Total cost per beneficiary (in US$)

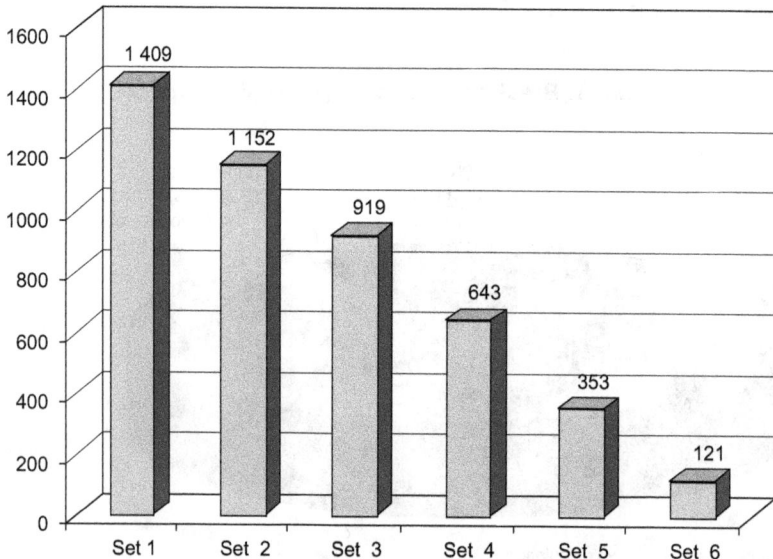

Source: Authors' own calculation.

Table 6. Total cost per beneficiary (in US$)

	Set 1 (2008-2013)	Set 2 (2009-2013)	Set 3 (2009-2013)	Set 4 (2011-2013)	Set 5 (2013)	Set 6 (2013)
Total beneficiary (as of June 2014)	8 281	35 079	13 168	69 924	34 831	45 493
Total non-cash transfer programme cost	1 167 040	2 068 755	2 600 201	2 719 968	708 493	1 252 512
Total programme cash transfers	10 500 137	38 353 074	9 504 922	42 218 205	11 579 857	4 272 284
Total programme costs	11 667 177	40 421 829	12 105 123	44 938 173	12 288 350	5 524 796
Total cost/beneficiary (in US$)	1 408.91	1 152.31	919.28	642.67	352.80	121.44
Annual total cost/ beneficiary (in US$)	281.78	288.08	229.82	321.33	352.80	121.44

Source: Authors' own calculation.

Note: 4Ps figures are translated into US dollars using an average exchange rate of Pts47.03 per $1 from 1998 to 2014.

However, when examining the data on an annual basis, the total cost per beneficiary tended to be higher on years when a new phase or set was implemented (2008, 2009, 2011 and 2013). Plausible reasons for this were presented above.

While the computed total and average cost per beneficiary for 4Ps cannot be compared to the cost per beneficiary of social transfers in other studies (even for similar programmes) because of the wide variations in the costs included in the calculations and the variations in the method of estimation, the information provided in table 7 elucidates how 4Ps implementation has fared in terms of cost efficiency.

The 4Ps' design features in terms of objectives, qualified beneficiaries and grants may have differences in some aspects with the various social programmes outlined in table 7. However, the cost per beneficiary of those social transfers does not show much disparity with that of 4Ps. Therefore, it can be deduced that the cost of implementing the latter programme falls within the accepted standard of cost efficiency.

Data envelopment analysis estimates of relative technical and cost efficiency

A summary of DEA estimates of relative technical efficiency (TE) and cost efficiency (CE) under variable returns to scale (VRS) assumptions per MOO is presented in table 8. It shows that most LGUs in the Set 1 phase of implementation

Table 7. Design features and costs of social transfers

Programme	Objective	Qualified beneficiaries	Grants	Cost per beneficiary
Bangladesh – BRAC Targeting the Ultra Poor (TUP)	To assist the ultra-poor population graduate from extreme poverty, get access to mainstream development programmes and establish sustainable livelihood improvement****	Ultra-poor households****	Intensive integrated support, including asset grants, skills development, personalized health-care support and social security****	$287 (total cost, including value of asset transferred plus monthly stipend to beneficiaries for 18 months)*
Ethiopia – Productive Safety Net Programme (SNP)	To increase access to safety net and disaster risk management systems, complementary livelihoods services and nutrition support for food insecure households in Ethiopia**	Chronically food insecure Ethiopians**	Cash transfers as wages for labour on small-scale public works projects**	$35 (annual cost)*
Malawi 2003/04 Targeted Input Programme (TIP)	To reduce poverty, hunger, starvation for all ultra-poor and labor-constrained households; to increase school enrolment and attendance of children living in target group household and invest in their health and nutrition status***	Ultra-poor household with high dependency ratio***	Monthly cash transfers that vary according to household size***	$7 per household (total cost)*

Table 7. *(continued)*

Programme	Objective	Qualified beneficiaries	Grants	Cost per beneficiary
Zambia - Pilot Social Cash Transfer Scheme	To reduce extreme poverty, hunger and starvation in the most destitute and incapacitated households**	Critically poor households and households with incapacitated member**	Monthly cash benefit**	US$144 per household**

Sources: * Devereux and Black (2007);

       ** www.ids.ac.uk/files/MakingCashCountfinal.pdf;

       *** www.fao.org/fileadmin/user_upload/p2p/Publications/MalawiSCT_ProductiveImpacts.pdf;

       **** www.ids.ac.uk/files/dmfile/2.1.Pahlowan2014-CFPR-TUPProgramBRACpptv229-apr-14.pdf.

Table 8. Summary of technical and cost-efficiency scores

Set	MOO	Average TE	Average CE
1	Caraga	1.00	0.66
1	Manay	1.00	0.66
1	Davao City	1.00	0.62
1	Malita	0.96	0.75
1	Sta Maria	0.93	0.70
2	Laak	0.90	0.35
2	Talaingod	0.80	0.34
2	Don Marcelino	0.87	0.35
2	Jose Abad Santos	0.88	0.35
2	Sarangani	0.87	0.35
2	Tarragona	1.00	0.34
3A	Compostela	0.88	0.83
3A	Island Garden City of Samal	0.87	0.85
3B	Braulio E Dujali	0.86	0.85
3B	Asuncion	0.86	0.85
3B	Carmen	0.86	0.85
3B	Kapalong	0.86	0.85
3B	New Corella	0.86	0.85

Table 8. *(continued)*

Set	MOO	Average TE	Average CE
3B	Panabo	0.86	0.85
3B	Sto Tomas	0.86	0.85
3B	Governor Generoso	1.00	0.86
3B	San Isidro (Oriental)	1.00	0.86
3C	Magsaysay	0.87	0.85
3D	Kiblawan	0.88	0.86
	Average	0.905	0.689

Source: Authors' own calculation.

posted technically efficient scores, while the technical efficiency scores of other MOOs in other sets were not far behind and relatively high, implying that implementation of 4Ps in the Davao Region was done efficiently. This may be attributed to the fact that most LGUs in the region were committed to the implementation of 4Ps at the local level by providing budget support for additional staff, logistics and other implementation requirements.

By contrast, it is noteworthy that there is a wide variation in cost-efficiency scores among MOOs in the different sets of implementation, with scores ranging from 34 per cent to 86 per cent. The variation in cost-efficiency scores among MOOs are shown in figure 3 by comparing the scores among MOOs by province. The most cost-efficient MOOs were in Davao del Norte, but it had the lowest technical efficiency scores, while the least cost-efficient MOOs were in Davao Oriental, which happened to be MOOs with the highest technical efficiency scores.

This finding suggests that not all MOOs implementing 4Ps with higher (or lower) technical efficiency scores would also be more (or less) cost-efficient in implementing the programme. The relevance of the trade-off between technical and cost-efficiency scores was noted by Grosh (1994, p. 46), who observed that "in several of the programmes, it appears that low administrative budgets might lead to deficient programme management", and that "spending more on administration with a given programme framework might lead to better service quality, better incidence or both". Accordingly, considering that most MOOs were given sufficient funds to implement the programme locally, there nonetheless would be MOOs that would need to spend more on administration costs, not only to deliver prompt service, but also to achieve the goals of the programme. MOOs that had higher administration costs typically were in areas far from the regional centre, resulting in

Figure 3. Comparison of average technical and cost-efficiency scores per province

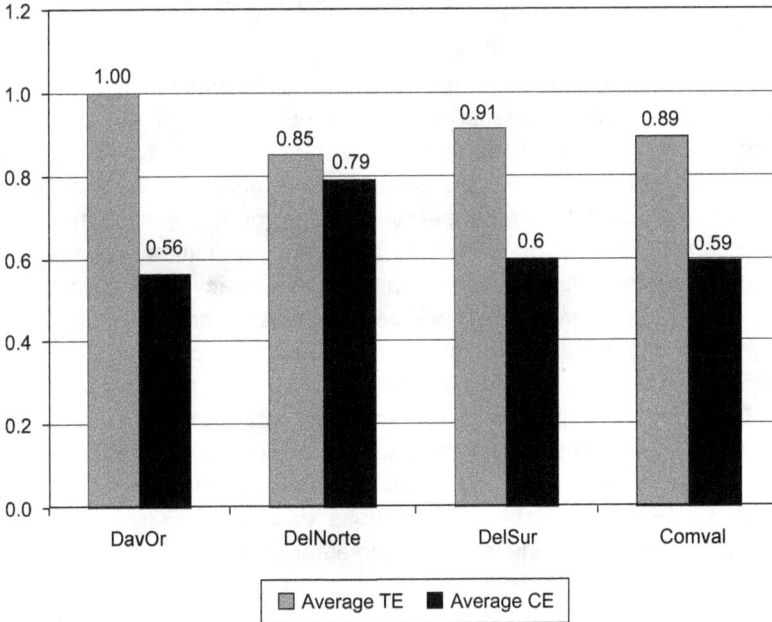

Source: Authors' own compilation.

higher logistical and travelling costs. This is the case for MOOs on the east coast of Davao Oriental (Tarragona, Manay and Caraga) and the far-flung MOOs of Davao del Sur (Don Marcelino, Jose Abad Santos and Sarangani), Davao del Norte (Talaingod) and Compostela Valley (Laak).

V. CONCLUSION

The empirical evaluation of the administrative efficiency of 4Ps at the regional level in the present paper is the first of its kind in terms of the cost assessment of implementing the programme. The design features of 4Ps include targeting methods and monitoring conditionalities, which is similar to the design characteristics employed in other countries that have adopted cash transfer programmes. However, the way a programme is delivered in terms of implementation varies considerably among programmes. In the 4Ps, the targeting of beneficiaries is centrally managed by the Philippines DSWD through the National Household Targeting Systems for Poverty Reduction (NHTS-PR), whereas the implementation of the programme is decentralized. Thus, assessing the cost of the programme at a regional level covers only from the implementation phase that commenced from the actual identification and registration of qualified beneficiaries to the actual delivery of cash through to the monitoring of conditionalities.

This study employed two methods of analysis: the estimation of CTRs and the estimation of technical and cost-efficiency scores using DEA. When computing CTRs of the programme, significant elements were revealed. On average, the largest proportion of the total spending per beneficiary is absorbed by the direct cash transfer, which is about 87 cents per one dollar (or peso) cash transferred to a beneficiary. Only 13 cents (per $1) was spent for programme delivery (including administration costs), capacity development, advocacy and monitoring, and evaluation, with a cost breakdown of 8.7 cents, 2.3 cents and 2 cents, respectively. This proportion of cost is equivalent to around 11.5 per cent of the total budget that is absorbed by the costs of different programme activities. When comparing CTRs of 4Ps with CTRs of the equivalent cash transfer programmes in Latin American countries with the same design features and cost structures (see table 1 for details), the 4Ps performance was similar to that of the Progresa programme in Mexico. This implies that as 4Ps were fashioned on those cash transfer programmes, while there might be some slight variation in implementation, cost efficiency was basically replicated by 4Ps.

Based on the computed activity cost shares, the largest proportion of the cost shares were devoted to the delivery of the programme (although most of that proportion was administrative costs). However, when taking the cost transfer ratio between non-transfer programme costs and the direct cash transfer costs, only 9 cents was spent on the non-transfer programme costs for every one dollar (or peso) transferred to a beneficiary. Consequently, this shows that, on average, 91.7 per cent of the budget for cash transfer is actually absorbed by the direct cash transfer. These findings conform with the principle proposed by Caldes, Coady and Maluccio (2006): "for a targeted and conditioned transfer programmes to be cost-effective at reducing poverty, they must be cost-efficient in terms of having low non-transfer costs".

As the cost data used in the analysis were limited only to the actual implementation activity, and did not include the targeting process of beneficiaries, as previously discussed, the study cannot fully refute common criticisms that a large proportion of the budget of cash transfer programmes is absorbed by administration costs instead of reaching the intended beneficiaries (Grosh, 1994). However, in a similar study, Grosh (1994, p. 46) pointed out that targeting costs are only a small part of total administrative costs and only equivalent to 0.4 to 8 per cent of total programme costs. It is thus prudent to deduce that the administrative costs of implementing 4Ps are relatively modest in terms of its share of the total transfer.

Moreover, when estimating the cost-efficiency scores using DEA, it was found that not all MOOs implementing 4Ps that had high relative technical efficiency scores translated to a more cost-efficient implementation of the programme, and vice versa. This finding corroborates the argument advanced by Grosh (1994). Furthermore, when analysing the relationship between cost-efficiency scores with that of the total cost per beneficiary, it was found that MOOs in Set 2 posting the highest total cost per beneficiary yielded lower cost-efficiency scores. The cost-efficiency scores for these MOOs in Set 2 were expected considering that most of these areas are geographically located farthest from the regional centre. Accordingly, more resources were devoted to monitoring conditionality, which essentially serves as a likely trade-off to cost efficiency. Similarly, LGUs in Set 3 that had a lower total cost per beneficiary posted higher cost-efficiency scores. Nonetheless, CTRs implied efficient use of resources with a greater proportion of the budget utilized in direct cash transfers, which also meant that MOOs implementing the programme were technically efficient. These results are consistent using CTR and DEA.

In sum, this study has established that the estimated average annual total cost per beneficiary of $265.88 is not dissimilar to the total cost per beneficiary of other cash transfer programmes with similar design features. Although these results are not comparable due to varying institutional circumstances, it can be concluded that 4Ps was reasonably well implemented by MOOs in a cost-efficient and technically efficient manner.

REFERENCES

Al-Jarrah, Idries Moh'd (2007). The use of DEA in measuring efficiency in Arabian banking. *Bank and Bank Systems*, vol. 2, No. 4, pp. 21-30.

Albert, Jose Ramon (2014). The costs and benefits of Pantawid Pamilya. *Rappler*, 3 December. Available from www.rappler.com/thought-leaders/76723-cost-benefits-pantawid-pamilya. Accessed 5 July 2015.

Caldes, Natalia, David Coady, and John Maluccio (2006). The cost of poverty alleviation transfer programs: a comparative analysis of three programs in Latin America. *World Development*, vol. 34, No. 5, pp. 818-837.

Caldes, Natalia, and John Maluccio (2005). The cost of conditional cash transfers. *Journal of International Development*, vol. 17, pp. 151-168.

Charnes, A., W.W. Cooper, and E. Rhodes (1978). Measuring the efficiency of decision making units. *European Journal of Operations Research*, vol. 2, No. 6, pp. 429-444.

Cheng, Xiaomei, Endre Bjorndal, and Mette Bjorndal (2014). Cost efficiency analysis based on DEA and StoNED models: case of Norwegian electricity distribution companies. Department of Business and Management Sciences Discussion Paper. Bergen, Norway: Norwegian School of Economics.

Coady, David, Raul Perez, and Hadid Vera-llamas (2005). Evaluating the cost of poverty alleviation transfer programmes: an illustration based on PROGRESA in Mexico. FCND Discussion Papers Brief, No. 199. Washington, D.C.: International Food Policy Research Institutute (IFPRI).

Davies, Mark (2009). DFID social transfers evaluation summary report. Department for International Development Working Paper, 31. Brighton, U.K.: University of Sussex, Institute of Development Studies Centre for Social Protection.

De Borger, Bruno, and Kristiaan Kerstens (1996). Cost efficiency of Belgian local governments: a comparative analysis of FDH, DEA and econometric approaches. *Regional Science and Urban Economics*, vol. 26, No. 2, pp. 145-170.

Devereux, Stephen, and S. Coll-Black (2007). Review of evidence and evidence gaps on the effectiveness an impacts of DFID-supported pilot social transfer schemes. DFID Evaluation Working Paper/Evaluation Report, A1/A3. Brighton: Institute of Development Studies.

Devereux, Stephen, and L. Pelham (2005). *Making Cash Count: Lessons from Cash Transfer Schemes in East and Southern Africa for Supporting the Most Vulnerable Children and Households*. London: Save the Children UK. Available from www.ids.ac.uk/files/MakingCashCountfinal.pdf. Accessed 30 June 2015.

Ellis, Frank, Stephen Devereux, and Phillip White (2009). *Social Protection in Africa*. Cheltenham, U.K.: Edward Elgar.

Fernandez, Luisa, and Rosechin Olfindo (2011). Overview of the Philippines' conditional cash transfer program: the *Pantawid Pamilyang Pilipino Program* (Pantawid Pamilya). Philippine Social Protection Note, No. 2 (Report No. 62879). Manila: World Bank Group and Australian Government Aid Program.

Fiorentino, Elizabetta, Alexander Karmann, and Michael Koetter (2006). The cost efficiency of German banks: a comparison of SFA and DEA. Discussion Paper Series 2: Banking and Financial Studies, No. 10. Frankfurt, Germany: Deutsche Bundesbank.

Fiszbien, Ariel, and others (2009). *Conditional Cash Transfers: Reducing Present and Future Poverty.* World Bank Policy Report, No. 47603. Washington, D.C.: World Bank. Available from https://openknowledge.worldbank.org/handle/10986/2597. Accessed 4 July 2015.

Giokas, D. (2002). The use of goal programming, regression analysis and data envelopment analysis for estimating efficient marginal costs of hospital services. *Journal of Multi-Criteria Decision Analysis*, vol. 11, No. 4-5, pp. 261-268.

Grosh, Margaret (1994). Administering targeted social programs in Latin America: from platitudes to practice. World Bank Regional and Sectoral Studies Series. Washington, D.C.

Handa, Sudhanshu, and Benjamin Davis (2006). The experiences of conditional cash transfer in Latin America and the Caribbean. *Development Policy Review*, vol. 24, No. 5, pp. 513-536.

Kakwani, Nanak, Fabio Veras Soares, and Hyun H. Son (2005). Conditional cash transfers in African countries. International Poverty Centre Working Paper, No. 9. Brasilia: United Nation Development Programme.

Karimzadeh, Majid (2012). Efficiency analysis by using data envelopment analysis model: evidence from Indian banks. *International Journal of Latest Trends in Finance and Economic Sciences*, vol. 2, No. 3, pp. 228-237.

O' Brien, Clare (2014). *A Guide to Calculating the Cost of Delivering Cash Transfers in Humanitarian Emergencies with Reference to Case Studies in Kenya and Somalia.* Working Paper, June. Oxford, U.K.: Oxford Policy Management.

Son, Hyun (2008). Conditional cash transfer programmes: an effective tool for poverty alleviation. ERD Policy Brief, No. 51. Manila: Asian Development Bank.

Steering Committee for the Review of Commonwealth/State Service Provision (SCRCSSP) (1997). Report on Commonwealth/State provision. Canberra: Australian Government Publishing Service.

Velarde, Rashiel, and Luisa Fernandez (2011). Welfare and distributional impacts of the *Pantawid Pamilyang Pilipino Program.* Philippine Protection Note, No. 3 (Report No. 63418). Manila: World Bank Group and Australian Government Aid Program.

Worthington, Andrew C. (2000). Cost efficiency in Australian nonbank financial institutions: a non-parametric approach. *Accounting and Finance*, vol. 40, No. 1, pp. 75-97.

ANNEX

Pantawid Pamilyang Pilipino Program costs in US dollars, per set and per year

Year	2008	2009			
Cost structures/set	Set 1	Set 1	Set 2	Set 3	Total
Programme costs	105 246	111 625	255 223	29 587	396 435
Total programme transfers	479 545	1 846 081	7 522 734	131 452	9 500 267
Cost transfer ratio	0.219	0.06	0.034	0.225	0.042
Cumulative cost transfer ratio/year	0.219	0.06	0.039	0.052	

Year	2010			
Cost structures/set	Set 1	Set 2	Set 3	Total
Programme costs	157 533	338 655	898 401	1 394 589
Total programme transfers	1 916 925	7 853 970	2 221 675	11 992 570
Cost transfer ratio	0.082	0.043	0.404	0.116
Cumulative cost transfer ratio/year	0.08	0.051	0.116	

Year	2011			
Cost structures/set	Set 1	Set 2	Set 3	Set 4	Total
Programme costs	187 087	349 547	904 783	685 602	2 127 019
Total programme transfers	2 012 620	7 508 752	2 698 263	9 355 706	21 575 341
Cost transfer ratio	0.093	0.047	0.335	0.073	0.099
Cumulative cost transfer ratio/year	0.093	0.056	0.118	0.099	

Year	2012			
Cost structures/set	Set 1	Set 2	Set 3	Set 4	Total
Programme costs	270 003	570 221	399 872	1 093 145	2 333 241
Total programme transfers	2 530 110	8 295 254	2 520 878	18 065 206	31 411 448
Cost transfer ratio	0.107	0.069	0.159	0.061	0.081
Cumulative cost transfer ratio/year	0.107	0.078	0.093	0.081	

Year	2013							Grand total-all sets
Cost structures/set	Set 1	Set 2	Set 3	Set 4	Set 5	Set 6	Total	
Programme costs	335 546	555 109	367 558	941 221	708 493	1 252 512	4 160 439	10 516 969
Total programme transfers	1 714 856	7 172 364	1 932 654	14 797 293	11 579 857	4 272 284	41 469 308	116 428 479
Cost transfer ratio	0.196	0.077	0.190	0.064	0.061	0.293	0.100	0.090
Cumulative cost transfer ratio/year	0.196	0.100	0.116	0.086	0.078	0.100		

Source: Authors' own compilation.

PURCHASE ORDER FORM

(Please type or print)

NAME: _____

POSITION: _____

ORGANIZATION: _____

ADDRESS: _____

_____

_____

_____

COUNTRY: _____ POSTCODE: _____

TELEPHONE: _____ FACSIMILE: _____ E-MAIL: _____

United Nations publications may be obtained from bookstores and distributors throughout the world. Please consult your bookstore or write to any of the following:

Customers in: America, Asia and the Pacific

E-mail: order@un.org
Web: un.org/publications
Tel: +1 703 661 1571
Fax: +1 703 996 1010

Mail Orders to:
United Nations Publications
PO Box 960
Herndon, Virginia 20172
United States of America

Customers in: Europe, Africa and the Middle East

United Nations Publication
c/o Eurospan Group
E-mail: info@eurospangroup.com
Web: un.org/publications
Tel: +44 (0) 1767 604972
Fax: +44 (0) 1767 601640

Mail Orders to:
United Nations Publications
Pegasus Drive, Stratton Business Park
Bigglewade, Bedfordshire SG18 8TQ
United Kingdom

For further information on publications in this series, please address your enquiries to:

Chief
Conference and Documentation Service Section
Office of the Executive Secretary
Economic and Social Commission for Asia and the Pacific
(ESCAP)
United Nations Building, Rajadamnern Nok Avenue
Bangkok 10200, Thailand

Tel: 66 2 288-1110
Fax: 66 2 288-1000
E-mail: escap-cdss@un.org

READERSHIP SURVEY

The Macroeconomic Policy and Financing for Development Division of ESCAP is undertaking an evaluation of the *Asia-Pacific Development Journal,* with a view to improving the usefulness of future publications to our readers. We would appreciate it if you could complete this questionnaire and return it, at your earliest convenience, to:

Director
Macroeconomic Policy and Financing for Development Division
ESCAP, United Nations Building
Rajadamnern Nok Avenue
Bangkok 10200, THAILAND
E-mail: escap-mpdd@un.org

QUESTIONNAIRE

	Excellent	Very good	Average	Poor
1. Please indicate your assessment of the *quality* of the publication in terms of:				
• presentation/format	4	3	2	1
• readability	4	3	2	1
• timeliness of information	4	3	2	1
• coverage of subject matter	4	3	2	1
• analytical rigour	4	3	2	1
• overall quality	4	3	2	1
2. How *useful* is the publication to your work?				
• provision of information	4	3	2	1
• clarification of issues	4	3	2	1
• its findings	4	3	2	1
• policy suggestions	4	3	2	1
• overall usefulness	4	3	2	1

3. **Please give examples of how this publication has contributed to your work:**

....

....

....

....

....

4. **Suggestions for improvement of similar publications:**

....

....

....

....

5. **Your background information, please:**

Name: ....

Title/position: ....

Institution:...

Office address: ....

....

Please use additional sheets of paper, if required, to answer the questions.
Thank you for your kind cooperation in completing this questionnaire.

ASIA-PACIFIC DEVELOPMENT JOURNAL
INSTRUCTIONS TO CONTRIBUTORS

Published by the Macroeconomic Policy and Financing for Development Division of the United Nations Economic and Social Commission for Asia and the Pacific, the *Asia-Pacific Development Journal* provides a platform for the exchange of ideas and experiences on development issues and concerns facing the region, and aims to stimulate policy debate and assist in the formulation of policy. Policy-oriented articles and original pieces of work, focusing on development issues and challenges relevant to the Asian and Pacific region, are welcomed in the *Journal*, which is published twice a year.

1.   MANUSCRIPTS

Authors are requested to provide copies of their manuscripts in English. Contributors should indicate in their covering letter to the Editorial Board that the material has not been previously published or submitted for publication elsewhere. The manuscripts should be typed, double-spaced, on one side of white A4 paper and the length should not exceed 30 pages. Manuscripts are accepted subject to editorial revision.

Since all manuscripts will be refereed by professionals in the field, the name(s) of the author(s), institutional affiliation(s) and other identifying information should be placed on the title page only, in order to preserve anonymity. The title page should contain the following: (a) title; (b) name(s) of the author(s); (c) institutional affiliation(s); (d) complete mailing address, telephone number, facsimile number and e-mail address of the author, or of the primary author in the case of joint authors; and (e) JEL classification and key words relevant to the article. The second page should contain the title, the name(s) of the author(s) and an abstract of approximately 150 words. Acknowledgement (if any) should appear after the abstract.

It is preferred that manuscripts be submitted by e-mail to the address below (if hard copies are submitted, kindly provide two copies of the manuscript to the address below). The preferred word-processing software is Microsoft Word. Once a manuscript is accepted for publication, the author(s) may be asked to submit electronic files of their manuscript, figures, tables and charts, as appropriate.

2.   FOOTNOTES AND QUOTATIONS

Footnotes, if any, should be numbered consecutively with superscript arabic numerals. They should be typed single-spaced and placed at the bottom of each page. Footnotes should not be used solely for citing references. Quotations should be double-spaced. A copy of the page(s) of the original source of the quotation, as well as a copy of the cover page of that source, should be provided.

3.   TABLES AND FIGURES

All tables and figures should be numbered consecutively with arabic numerals. Each table should be typed double-spaced. Tables and figures should be planned to fit the proportions of the printed page. Full information on the source(s) should appear below the table/figure, followed by notes, if any, in lower-case letters.

4.   REFERENCES

Authors should ensure that there is a complete reference for every citation in the text. References in the text should follow the author-date format, followed, if necessary, by page numbers, for example, Becker (1964, pp. 13-24). List only those references that are actually cited in the text or footnotes. References, listed alphabetically, should be typed double-spaced on a separate page in the following style:

Desai, Padma, ed. (1883). *Marxism, Central Planning, and the Soviet Economy.* Cambridge, MA: MIT Press.

Husseini, Rana (2007). Women leaders attempt to bridge East–West cultural divide. *Jordan Times*, 9 May.

Krueger, Alan B., and Lawrence H. Summers (1987). Reflections on the inter-industry wage structure. In *Unemployment and the Structure of Labour Markets*, Kevin Lang and Jonathan S. Leonard, eds. London: Basis Blackwell.

Moran, Theodore H., and Gerald T. West, eds. (2005). *International Political Risk Management*, vol. 3, *Looking to the Future*. Washington, D.C.: World Bank.

Sadorsky, P. (1994). The behaviour of U.S. tariff rates: comment. *American Economic Review*, vol. 84, No. 4, September, pp. 1097-1103.

Salagaev, Alexander (2002). Juvenile delinquency. Paper presented at the Expert Group Meeting on Global Priorities for Youth. Helsinki, October.

Stiglitz, Joseph, and others (2006). *Stability with Growth: Macroeconomics, Liberalization and Development*. Initiative for Policy Dialogue Series. Oxford: Oxford University Press.

United Kingdom, Department for Education and Skills (2007). *Care Matters: Time for Change*. London: The Stationery Office. Available from www.official-documents.gov.uk.

For further details on referencing, please refer to the editorial guidelines at: www.unescap.org/sites/default/files/apdj_editorial_guidelines.pdf. The Editorial Board of the *Asia-Pacific Development Journal* would like to emphasize that papers need to be thoroughly edited in terms of the English language, and authors are kindly requested to submit manuscripts that strictly conform to the attached editorial guidelines.

Manuscripts should be sent to:
Chief Editor, *Asia-Pacific Development Journal*
Macroeconomic Policy and Financing for Development Division
Economic and Social Commission for Asia and the Pacific
United Nations Building
Rajadamnern Nok Avenue
Bangkok 10200
Thailand
Tel: 66 2 288-1902
Fax: 66 2 288-1000; 66 2 288-3007
E-mail: escap-mpdd@un.org